THE COMICAL PILGRIM

THE COMICAL PILGRIM

ANONYMOUS

ISBN: 978-93-5614-277-0

Published: 1722

LECTOR HOUSE LLP
E-MAIL: lectorpublishing@gmail.com

G Thorton Scul.

THE COMICAL PILGRIM;

OR, TRAVELS
OF A CYNICK PHILOSOPHER,

THRO' THE MOST WICKED PARTS
OF THE WORLD,

Namely,

ENGLAND,		IRELAND,
WALES,	} {	and
SCOTLAND,		HOLLAND.

WITH

His *Merry* Observations on the *English* Stage, Gaming-Houses, Poets, Beaux, Women, Courtiers, Politicians, and Plotters. *Welsh* Clergy, Gentry, and Customs. *Scotch* Manners, Religion, and Lawyers. *Irish* Ceremonies in their Marriages, Christenings, and Burials. And *Dutch* Government, Polity, and Trade.

BEING
A General SATYR on the Vices and Follies of the Age.

THE SECOND EDITION.

1722

THE PREFACE.

s Prefaces now are become common to every Production of the Press, I am resolv'd to be in the Fashion likewise, to let my Reader understand that I am not an Ascetick, or one of those devout Pilgrims, who will travel on Foot to see the holy Sepulchre, the Chapel of Loretto, or some strange Relique; but a comical merry Traveller that would take a Perigrination, on Horseback or by Water, beyond the Devil's Arse i'th' Peak, to see the Religion, Customs, and Manners of foreign People, as well as knowing those of my own Country; contrary to the Sentiments of Claudian, who mentions it as a Happiness, for Birth, Life, and Burial, to be all in one Parish.

Some Pilgrims may brag of their having seen a Vial full of the Virgin Mary's Milk; another Vial full of Mary Magdalen's repenting Tears; the Pummel of the Sword with which the Ear of Malchus, the high Priest's Servant, was cut off; the Bill of the Cock which crow'd after Saint Peter had deny'd his Master, set in Silver; an Ell Flemish of the Cord with which Judas hang'd himself; a Linnen Apron worn by our Saviour's hæmorrhoidal Patient; a Piece of the seemless Garment, for which the Jewish Soldiers cast Lots; one of Saint John the Baptist's Eye-Teeth, set in Gold; Saint Paul's Cloak, which he left at Troas, never the worse for wearing; and talk also of their often meeting with the wandering Jew in their Travels; these, I say, were Curiosities I valu'd not seeing; but in all Places wherever I came, I made general Observations on the Folly and Vices of the Inhabitants, thereby to correct my own Manners, which, indeed, is a very fine Thing, in either Man or Beast.

In Order hereto, I have travell'd in three Parts of the World; namely, Europe, Africa, and America; and tho' Wickedness reigns in all Parts of the World, yet must I needs say, that it is not so predominate in any Place as in England, Wales, Scotland, Ireland, and Holland; where it is as hard to find Religion, Honesty and Virtue walk Hand in Hand, as it was for Diogenes to find an honest Woman in Athens. This Dearth of good Manners oblig'd me, with the abovesaid Philosopher to turn Cynick; and if by these Lucubrations, I can so far put Folly and Vice, out of Countenance, as to reclaim a wicked Age, it is all the Author desires for the Fatigue of taking a Pilgrimage, by Land and Sea, of above Eleven Thousand Miles, which is more than half the Circumference of the whole Earth.

CONTENTS

THE COMICAL PILGRIM,
OR,
TRAVELS THRO' ENGLAND.

s *London* is the Metropolis, or capital City in the World, for Pride, Luxury, and all other Vices; I was very curious of making some Observations on them. In Order hereto, I frequented several Taverns, where was nothing but Drunkenness, and young Rakes vomiting about the Room, and in their *Bacchanalian* Frolicks (which made them think, with *Copernicus*, the Earth turn'd round) breaking Pipes and Glasses, to inflame a great Reckoning to a larger Sum. I also haunted Jelly-Houses, where was no other Diversion, than seeing proud conceited Coxcombs eating Jellies, with a gilded Pap-Spoon, for Provocation to venerial Sports; which by lighting on a Fire-Ship, might bring them to the Charge and Misery of Pills, Bolusses, Electuaries, and Diet-Drinks; so that these gallanting Stallions, need no other Injunction of Penance, from the most rigid Confessor: And at every common Gaming-House about Town, the Gamesters are as lavishing of their Oaths and Curses, as they are at the Groom Porter's. One is cursing the Dice, another biting his Thumbs, and another scratching where it doth not itch, whilst others are flourishing their Swords in the midst of twenty G——d——s, to have their lost Money again.

Think I to myself, the frequenting of these Places, will return to no better Account towards a Reformation of bad Manners, than if a Man should go to a Bawdy-House, to keep out of ill Company. So having heard that a deal of good Manners and Morality, might be learnt, in seeing Plays acted on the *English* Stage; I then flung away many a Half Crown at the Theatres in *Bridges-Street*, and *Lincoln's Inn Fields*, but by the immoral, profane, and impious Expressions us'd in the dramatick Writings, whether tragical or comical, I could reckon the Play-Houses, no other than Schools of Iniquity, the Sinks of all Wickedness, and Markets for the Devil. 'Tis out of doubt, that even the Theatres of *Greece* and *Rome*, under Heathenism, were less obnoxious and offensive, yet nevertheless they stood condemn'd by the primitive Fathers, and general Councils.

The detestable lewd Expressions in the *English* Plays, can do no less than debauch the Minds, and corrupt the Manners of the Audience; but it must needs strike every good *Christian* with Horror, to hear on the Stage Almighty God blasphem'd, his Providence question'd and deny'd, his Name prophan'd, his Attributes ascrib'd to sinful Creatures, and even to heathen Gods, his holy Word burlesqu'd, and treated as a Fable, his Grace made a Jest of, his Ministers despis'd, Conscience laugh'd at, Religion ridicul'd, the Catholick Faith and Doctrine expos'd, the sincere Practice of Religion, represented as the Effect of Vapours and Melancholly, Virtue discountenanc'd, Vice encourag'd, Evil treated as Good, and Good as Evil; and all this highly aggravated, by being done in cool Blood, upon Choice and Deliberation.

The Infidelity and Loosness of the present Age, is very much owing to the Play-Houses, where the Infection of most abominable Wickedness, spreads among the Spectators, from the Lady in the Front or Side-Box, to the tawdry Chambermaid in upper Gallery. Men and Women who frequent the Theatre, are, instead of learning Virtue, surrounded with inordinate Temptations, which incite them to unlawful Desires and Actions, which soon end in the utter Ruin, both of Body and Soul. Where Lewdness is represented, in all the Dresses that can vitiate the Imagination, and fasten upon the Memory; and where Pride and Falshood, Malice and Revenge, Injustice and Immodesty, Contempt of Marriage, and false Notions of Honour are recommended, no Good can be learn'd, either by old or young; and this not among *Mahometans* and *Infidels*, not at *Rome* and *Venice*, not in *France* and *Spain*, but in a *Protestant* Country, and upon the *English* Stage, without any Fear that the Judgments of God will fall upon them. The *Players* exposing (as they pretend they do) Formality, Humour, and Pedantry, is not an equivalent for their insulting sacred Things, and their promoting to so high a Degree, the Prophaneness and Debauchery of the Nation.

Those who frequent the Play-House, say (to palliate the sin) a great deal of Morality is to be learnt from Plays; but I cannot perceive what good Morals can be obtained from such Expressions as these. "Sure, if Woman had been ready created, the Devil, instead of being kickt down to Hell, had been married. *Leonora*'s Charms turn Vice to Virtue, Treason into Truth; Nature, who has made her the supreme Object of our Desires, must needs have design'd her the Regulater of our Morals. She's mad with the Whimsies of Virtue, and the Devil. Damn'd Lies, by *Jupiter* and *Juno*, and the rest of the Heathen Gods and Goddesses; for I remember I paid two Guineas for swearing *Christian* Oaths last Night." As may be seen in several of the comick Writers. However, the Admirers of the Stage must have some Excuse for their Folly, and thus the Devil too, to support Vice, hangs out the Colours of Virtue. Again, we cannot see what Morality can be learnt in, there Expressions in the following Tragedies of *Œdipus* and *Theodosius*.

> *Tho' round my Bed the Furies plant their Charms,*
> *I'll break 'em, with* Jocasta *in my Arms:*
> *Claspt in the Folds of Love, I'll wait my Doom,*
> *And act my Joys, tho' Thunder shakes the Room.* Act 2.
>
> *Nor shall I need a Violence to wound,*
> *The Storm is here that drives me on the Ground,*
> *Sure Means to make the Soul and Body part,*
> *A burning Fever, and a broken Heart.* Act 5. Scene 2.

In which Lines abovesaid may be seen the Lover pursuing his Amours in Defiance of Heaven; and *Varanes* dying a natural Death, or else he had been so wicked, as to have laid violent hands on himself. Neither are the *Greek* and *Latin* Dramatists without their prophane Flights, and wicked Rants: Nay, hear how *Augustin*, that great Father of the Church, in these Words, *Non omnino per hanc turpitudinem verba ista commodius discuntur, sed per hæc verba turpitudo ista confidentius perpetratur.* Confes. lib. 1. cap. 16. condemns the following Lines of *Terence's* Eunuch, Act 3. Scene 5.

> *Suspectans tabulam quandam pictam, ubi inerat pictura hæc, Jovem*
> *Quo pacto Danaæ misisse aiunt quondam in gremium imbrem aureum*
> *Egomet quoque id spectare cœpi, &c.*

In short, no good Manners can be acquir'd on the *English* Stage, by seeing an Actor going a Tiptoe, in Derision of mincing Dames; sometimes speaking full-mouth'd, to mock the Country Clowns; and sometimes upon the Tip of the Tongue, to scoff the Citizen? that thus, by the Imitation of all ridiculous Gestures, or Speeches, in all Kinds of Vocations, they may provoke Laughter. When Stages were first set up in *Rome*, it was accounted infamous to frequent them; and in *England*, Players, both Men and Women, are reckon'd so scandalous, that tho' they stile themselves his Majesty's Servants, yet the Statute Law terms them Vagabonds: "Indeed they are so infamously wicked, that one who never saw them in this Life, may nevertheless at the Resurrection, know their Bodies and Souls are Fellows; insomuch that as the Play-House in *Drury-Lane* has been burnt once already, it would be a Mercy rather than a Judgment, if God vouchsafed to smite them once again."

The Audience in the Upper-Gallery is generally compos'd of Lawyers Clerks, Valets de Chambre, Exchange-Girls, Chamber-Maids, and Skip-kennels, who at the last Act are let in *gratis*, in Favour to their Masters being Benefactors to the Devil's Servants. The Middle-Gallery is taken up by the midling Sort of People, as Citizens, their Wives, and Daughters, and other Jilts, who make it their Business to let out their Commodities in Fee-tail, to the first Cully she picks up, after Play is over, for a small Treat, and twelve Pence dry. The Boxes are fill'd with Lords and Ladies, who give Money to see their Follies expos'd by Fellows as wicked as themselves. And the Pit, which lively represents the Pit of Hell, is cramm'd with those insignificant Animals called Beaux, whose Character nothing but Wonder and Shame can compose; for a modern Beaux (you must know) is a pretty neat, phantastical Outside of a Man; a well digested Bundle of costly Vanities; and you may call him a Volume of methodical Errata's bound in a gilt Cover. He's a curiously wrought Cabinet full of Shells and other Trumpery, which were much better quite empty, than so emptily full. He's a Man's Skin full of Prophaness, a Paradise full of Weeds; a Heaven cramm'd full of Devils, or *Satan's* Bed-Chamber, hung with Arras of God's own making. He can be thought no better than a *Promethean* Man; at best but a Lump of animated Dirt kneaded into Humane Shape; and if he has any such Thing as a Soul, it seems to be patch'd up with more Vices than are Patches in a poor *Spaniard's* Cloak. His general Employment is to scorn all Business, but the Study of the Modes and Vices of the Times; and you may look upon him as upon the painted Sign of a man hung up in the Air, only to be toss'd to and fro with every Wind of Temptation and Vanity. As for his Apparel, he endeavours to that all should appear new about him, except his Vices and Religion; he's too much in Love with these to change them; besides, the latter of them he cannot change, because he never had any. When you look upon his Cloaths, you will be apt to say, he wears his Heaven upon his Back; and truly ('tis much to be fear'd) you see as much of it there, as He ever shall. He is trick'd up in such Gauderies, as if he was resolv'd to make his Body a Lure for the Devil; and with this Bravery would make a Bait should tempt the Tempter to fall in Love with him. By this Variety of Fashions he goes nigh to cheat his Creditors; who for this Reason, dare never swear him to be the same Man they formerly had to deal withal. His Draper may very well be afraid to lose him in a Labyrinth of his own Cloth, which fits, or hangs (shall I say?) for the most part so loosely about him, as if it were ever ready to fly away, for Fear of a Bailiff.

His Language and Discourse are altogether suitable to his Garb and Habit, all affected and apish, but indeed, far more vile, sinful, and abominable. When he talks, why then his Time-observing Hand and Foot do so point, accent, and adorn all his phantastick Flourishes, that his Words are often as much lost in his Actions, as his Sense in his Words: Withal using foolish Expressions, as stab my Vitals, run me through the *Diaphragma*, pasitively (not positively) it is so and so; speaking as effeminately, and Molly-like, as the *Ischnotes*, who say, as you may see in *Lilly*'s Grammar, *Nync* for *Nunc*, *Tync* for *Tunc*. By Degrees he steps from Idleness and Emptiness, Foolery and Drollery, to Scurrility and Obloquy; so that if his black Breath could blow out, or eclipse those Lights that shine brightest, we should not have one Star left in Virtue's Heaven; and those Lights which were once sent into the World, to guide him timely and truly out of it into a better, he first endeavours to extinguish, that so he may, without Check or Shame, wander thro' all the Works of Darkness into Hell. Alas! he sees no such Loveliness in the Things above, as may oblige him to the submissive Courtship of saying his Prayers below; and yet is so confident to enjoy Heaven at last; as if he thought God would be beholden to him for accepting his Blessings; or (as some foolish Lovers take Occasion to double their Addresses from the Unkindness of a coy Mistress) God would the more earnestly importune him to be sav'd, the more disdainfully he looks upon Salvation. If ever he appears at Church, it is but to meditate upon the Ladies, as they sit in their Sunday's Beauties; and then he returns from the House of God, as most who go thither with no better Intentions, nay ten Times more an *Athiest* than he went.

The Theatre in the *Hay-Market* is his sole Delight, where half a Guinea is given for an *Italian* Song, sung in a new Opera by some foreign Eunuch, or Jilt, with such Quivering, that the Words are lost and confounded with more affected Noise than Harmony. Or else he passes his Time away (as above hinted) at the Play-Houses in *Drury-Lane*, or *Lincoln's-Inn Fields*, to ogle an impudent Actress, or some female Dancer, who crane's her Neck with such various Motions, that one would think she was going to break it without the Assistance of a Hangman. Or if he is not at these Places of Pollution and Wickedness, the Tavern he then makes his Exchange; where he endeavours to drink himself so far into a Beast, as if it was his Design to become thereby incapable of Damnation, except he be forc'd to sleep out the last Night's Intemperance; and thinks himself a Champion, when he can kick two down Stairs at once, the Drawer and his Bottle; and sound the Alarm to the Skirmish, in a loud Peal of new-fashion'd Curses. After all is done there, he walks the Streets as light in his Head, as his Purse; and much oftner salutes the Pavement than the Passengers. The Beau hates no Name so much as that of a *Christian*, he is afraid it would make him melancholy: He travels over the wide World of Sin, till he hath as little Money as Religion, and no more Credit than Money; whereby he is usually at last constrain'd either to lie hid, and so become his own Prisoner, or to pawn his Body to the Marshal of the *King's Bench* Prison in *Southwark*, or the Warden of the *Fleet*, for his Chamber; or else, to become a Citizen of the World, and so at last is every where at Home, because he is indeed at Home no where. In fine, I never saw an affected Beau have any Bravery; which makes me think they are related to a certain Attorney, who once resenting my sending an affronting Letter to his Sweetheart, had not the Courage to draw his Tilter, when I *ex tempore* spoke to him the following Lines:

> *Know, Sir, that I was really bred and born*
> *To lash the Vices of the Age; and sworn*
> *To lampoon* Beaux, *and* Jilts; *and to condemn*
> *What* Pulpits, *nor the* Stage *dare not contemn:*
> *So Anger,* Frank, *can no Redress afford,*
> *For to defend my Pen, see here's my Sword.*

Now think I with myself, if this be the Way of *London*, Drinking, Gaming, and Whoring; I'll e'en retire into the Country, where I thought was more Simplicity and Honesty among the Rusticks than the Citizens; but I found myself mistaken, for going to *Deptford*, I perceiv'd as much Drunkenness among the *Tarpaulins*, as among the Admirers of *Geneva*, at the *Frenchman*'s Bob-Shop, or *dirty-Face Dick* in the *Strand*; but however, the *Tarpaulin*'s *Froes of this Place, as well as at* Wapping, *are pretty virtuous, thro' their Husband's making them go without Smocks, to prevent their Neighbours from taking up their Wives Linnen.* From hence, I went to *Greenwich-Park*, where I found as many Assignations made betwixt Whore and Cully, as in *St. James's*, or *Hyde-Park*. Here was as much Lying by the Fops in Praise of their Mistresses, as is among Lawyers; as much Flattering, as there is at Court; and as much Dissembling, as in a *Presbyterian* or *Anabaptist* Meeting-House; a Folly, which I must own, I have been formerly guilty of myself, when I sent to a young Gentlewoman this amorous Petition, for Flattery is the only Bait to decoy the coyest Virgin in *England*.

> *Harmonious Numbers now my Muse does find,*
> *To sing the choicest of your precious Kind.*
> *Thy Wit, as well as Beauty, lovely Dame,*
> *Who first my Breast, and more than Wealth, or Fame,*
> *Exerts my Soul, and is my constant Aim.*
> *The genuine Blushes that your Cheeks adorn,*
> *Were ravish'd from the Rose, or crimson Morn;*
> *The* Persian *Insects labr'ing, wrought with Care*

The slender silken Threads that form your Hair;
The clear, quick Lustre of your piercing Eyes,
Was shot from Di'monds, or the spangled Skies;
Vermilion Coral *left its ozie Bed,*
To flush your balmy Lips with glowing Red;
To frame your Teeth, choice Pearls did crowding come,
Each from its secret Cell in Ocean's *Womb:*
Arabian *Sweets did all their Stores transfer,*
And fed from Home, to breath in you, bright Star.
Eden *once flourish'd like your blooming Face,*
Your Shape, your Mein, and unaffected Grace,
From Heav'n the first of Females once possess'd,
Created as a Pattern to the rest:
From Spring your Gaiety, from calmest Brooks
Was wafted the Sereneness of your Looks;
Sweet Philomel, *as she departing, sung,*
Bequeath'd the Musick of your silver Tongue;
The Down of Swans, and Lillies, or the gay
And fragrant Bloom that crowns the youthful May,
To frame your Skin, did gracefully unite
Their yielding Softness, and unblemish'd White:
The vast Cerulean Sky, Earth, Sea, and Air,
Did then combin'd, and various Stores prepare
(At Heaven's commanding Call) to frame you fair.
They fram'd you of their rarest Treasures joyn'd,
And in the Mould an Angel's Soul unshrin'd
Therefore, fair Virgin, whose most dazling Charms
Can Saints and Anchorites bring to your Arms,
Let us this Day, for it's a Law divine,
Offer our mutual Hearts on Cupid's Shrine;
Revel, whilst living, in the Joys of Love,
Like thund'ring Jove, and other Gods above;
For if we slight bright Venus *while we've Breath,*
There'll be no Thoughts of loving after Death.

But being soon tir'd of *Greenwich,* I proceeded on my Pilgrimage to *Gravesend,* where, (and at *Stroud, Rochester,* and *Chatham*) the Vintners, Innkeepers, and Victuallers, are more extortioning than any Pawn-Broker, who has the Honesty to take no more than *Cent. per Cent.* for what Money they lend. Hereupon, bidding adieu to the County of *Kent,* I rambled through the County of *Surry;* but it being Assize-Time when I arriv'd at *Kingston* upon *Thames,* I found I was leap'd out of the Fryingpan into the Fire, for Provisions and Lodging were then as dear as a Suit of Law in *Chancery;* so that I rid forthwith into the County of *Sussex,* where I saw nothing but a Parcel of Bumpkins and Milk-Wenches returning all home, as drunk as *David's* sow, from a Country-Wake. Thence, I went into *Hampshire,* where Rusticks are as fat as their Hogs and as liquorish as those who buy their Honey. In this County is *Southampton,* where the Sword of Sir *Bevis* is held in as much

Veneration by the Towns People, as a Piece of Paper worn by 'Prentice-Boys, and Servant-Wenches on *Valentine*'s Day. Hence, I went to *Portsmouth*, betwixt which Place and Hell, the Soldiers garrison'd here say, there is but only a Sheet of brown Paper; however, it is honour'd by giving the Title of a Dutchess to *Squintabella, alias* Madamoiselle *Louise de Querouaille.* At this Sea-port, crossing the Water, I reached at the Distance of three Leagues, the *Isle of Wight*, and proceeded to *Carisbrook* Castle, which inwardly, (as well as outwardly) is much out of Repair, especially the Room in which King *Charles* I. was confin'd a Prisoner, a little before the horrid Murder perpetrated on him, the then prevailing Party, who under a Stratocracy or Army-Power, brought him to the Block, and then conspir'd to overthrow the well settled Constitution of this Kingdom with Anarchy, and Confusion which unparalleled Piece of Villany incited me to write *ex tempore* on the Wall of that fatal Place, the following Lines.

> *What dismal Horror, and as dismal Gloom,*
> *Invades the hallow'd Silence of this Room!*
> *Where Majesty in Mourning sat, to wait*
> *The wreched News of his more wretched Fate;*
> *Curst Spawn of Schism! to give the fatal Shock,*
> *Which sent a King a Martyr from the Block.*
> *The barbarous Act, which smote his Royal Head,*
> *Our Calendars shall ever die with Red;*
> *To paint the Overthrow of th' Church and State,*
> *In the rebellious Times of Forty Eight.*
> *My Muse, with the shrill Eccho of these Walls,*
> *For Vengeance on the bloody Nation calls;*
> *And weeps, till fruitful* Albion *is freed*
> *From the* Fanaticks *pestilential Breed;*
> *An Offspring sprung from that most odious Race,*
> *Whose Hanging would the* Tripple-Tree *disgrace.*
> *The Royal Captive here remained in Tears,*
> *Till* Bradshaw *doom'd a Period to his Years;*
> *But now the injur'd Saint in Peace does dwell,*
> *While those that judg'd him, burning are in Hell.*

Getting cross the Water again, from this dismal Isle, I no sooner set Foot upon *Terra firma*, but I made the best of my Way for *Berkshire*; where I took a Survey of *Windsor* Castle, and then thought myself as well Qualify'd as any Knight of the Garter, to take a Pilgrimage whither I pleas'd: So with a full Body, and an empty Stomach, (for you must know, we Pilgrims live not very daintily) I went into *Wiltshire*, where I as much admired the Cathedral of *Salisbury*, (as an Antiquary, doth an old Tomb; who will go forty Miles, and more to see it) because it contain'd as many Windows about it, as a *German* Countess did once Children in her Womb, which were just three hundred sixty five, the precise Number of Days in the Year, unless it happens to be *Bissextile* or Leap-Year, which has one Day more. Hence, I went with a light Heart, and a thin Pair of Breeches into *Dorsetshire*; where being nothing remarkable to take Notice of, it came into my Noddle to make the following Acrostick on Nothing.

> *N othing was the first Matter made the World;*
> *O n Man e'er since nothing but Plagues are hurl'd.*
> *T he Tye of Wedlock's nothing but a Snare:*
> *H onour's like nothing but the empty Air.*
> *I rishmen are nothing but Fools void of Sense*
> *N othing is Sin but publick Insolence.*
> *G old! Gold! and nothing else quits the Offence.*

Next, I went a pilgramaging into *Devonshire*, which might be properly call'd *Devilshire*, for seeing how the Inhabitants would eat White-Pots red hot in a Manner, a Stranger would be apt to conclude, they came from whence they have nothing else for their Food but Brimstone and Fire. Hereupon, I galloped strait into *Cornwal*, a County very plentiful of Wood-Cocks, not only flying in the Air, but you should also see them smoaking or tipling in every Chimney-Corner, in Winter. Thence, I rambled into *Somersetshire*, where, at the *Bath*, I saw so much Whoredom committed, that I thought the Men, or Women neither had Occasion to wash themselves in hot Water, when their Bodies were all on Fire before; unless it was to make an Experiment of that Aphorism in Physick, which says, one Heat drives out another. Not liking this Place, I took a Pilgrimage (I can't say Tour, or Progress, because Pilgrims are not Noblemen) into *Gloucestershire*, where I saw the Sins of the People were as red as the Scarlet they die; so I soon shook the Dust off my Shoes, as a Testimony against their Wickedness, and went to *Oxon*.

No sooner was I enter'd into *Oxfordshire*, but I was in as longing a Condition, as the big-bellied Woman was for a bite of a Butcher's Arm, to see the most famous University of *Oxford*; thinking that in that Academy and Nursery of Learning, I should see Piety, and Virtue, climb up to the very Apex of Glory; but too soon were my Hopes frustrated, for instead of Religion and good Manners, I beheld nothing but Irreligion and Prophaneness; for the Scholars were so far from being religious, that they were asham'd of nothing so much as that any should have the Charity to think them so. They seem'd to cry out upon *Eve*, for a lazy and dull Sinner; whilst in every Oath they loudly swore, that Soul not worth damning, that could not sin without a Temptation. By their horrible and hideous Oaths they shew'd, as if indeed they had this desperate Design upon Almighty God, to render his sacred Name odious to the World, by taking it often in their profane Mouths. Their chief Delight was to dwell upon the sore Place of an obscene Poem; at the same Time never commending the Poet, but for his Infirmities. Those Sparks call'd Gentlemen Commoners, were so fantastical and prodigal, that they walk'd as if they went in a Frame; next as if both Head and every Member of them turn'd upon Hinges. Every Step they took, presented me with a perfect Puppet-Play; and *Rome* itself could not in an Age have shew'd more Anticks, than one of these Blades was able to imitate in half an Hour. Here those who have Money enough allow'd them by their Friends, learn first of all to make Choice of their boon Companions, how to rail at the Statutes, and break all good Orders; how to wear a gaudy Suit, and a torn Gown; to curse their Tutors by the Name of *Baal*'s Priests, and to sell more Books in half an Hour, than they had bought them in a Year; to forget the second

Year what, perhaps for want of Acquaintance with the Vices of the Place, they were forc'd for a Pass-Time to learn in the first, and then they think they have Learning enough for them and their Heirs for ever.

Thought I to my self, if this is *Oxford*, the Devil take the Collegians and Citizens too, for there was never Barrel the better Herring betwixt either of 'em; one was full as bad as the other, so I e'en made the best of my Way into *Buckinghamshire*, where, at *Eaton* College, finding the Scholars to have more Guts than Brains, and less Learning and good Manners than either of the two, *Utrum horum mavis accipe*, as you may see in *Syntaxis*. I rambl'd through *Oxfordshire*, again into *Worcestershire*, where I observ'd nothing material, but poor Skeletons of Men and Women, knitting Mittins and Stockings; and Children, both Boys and Girls, smoaking Tobacco, in Pipes as black as their Faces, and about an Inch in Length, for a Breakfast. Hence I went into *Herefordshire*, where I thought myself under the same Punishment, as *Tantalus* was when in Hell, for the Hedge-Rows all along the Roads, being full of Apple-Trees, the Apples would bob at my Mouth, but I could not catch 'em, which I think was tantalizing me with a Vengeance.

I had not been long in this County, before I steer'd my Course for *Warwickshire*, where in the City of *Coventry*, I was shew'd the wooden Picture of a Cobler, which (as the People told me) was made to perpetuate the Memory of one of *Crispin*'s Occupation, whose Mouth watering to peep thro' his Garret Window, to see the Lady *Godiva*'s *Ay-forsooth*, as she rid naked on Horseback through the City, to release the Inhabitants from heavy Taxes laid upon them by her Husband *Leofric*, he was struck blind for his Sauciness of presuming to look at lac'd Mutton. But above all, this County glories much in that it gave Birth to *Guy* Earl of *Warwick*, who killing a fierce dun Cow upon *Dunmoor-Heath*, by *Dunchurch*, both which Places (I suppose) take their Names from this heroick Bravery; and for this Piece of Service and other Exploits, as killing a wild Boar; his Memory is also still perpetuated, as well as the abovesaid Cobler's, in many Victuallers Signs, to this Day.

Next, going into *Northamptonshire*, and Night beginning to creep upon me, I began to be mighty Melancholly, as being all alone; but as good Luck would have it, I overtook a Cordwainer, who (as he told me) was newly recover'd from a sad Mischance; for walking carelesly one Day, he happen'd to have a Fall, and to squat his Breech upon a Hedge-Hog, which he carry'd away as cleverly (it clinging to his Buttocks) as if he had sate upon a Ball of his Wax. Whether there is a Sympathy between a Shoemaker's Tail, and the Skin of an Urchin, or whether the Bristles of the Creature enter'd the Pores of his Backside, I list not to decide that Controversy now; but however, the Mortal complain'd, that it was an uneasy Cushion, and that that Spinny of Awls, had made a Cullender of his Backside. But being not much concern'd at the Cerebrosity of his scievy Bum, the Eyelet-Holes whereof being not very deep, we went together, till we came to a Church, standing like an Ace, and moping by itself, at some Distance from a little Village; which, whether it ran from the Parish, or the Parish from it, I was not then inform'd; though I have most Reason to suspect the latter, in Regard as to outward Appearance the weak Constitution of the Fabrick seem'd not much to be addicted to run. It seem'd to be very crazy, and had a Muffler of Ivy, which I presume was instead of Crutches; for whereas that feeble Vegetable is usually upheld by the Walls it clings to, I believe it was a Buttress here to support the Walls. But having sadden'd our Aspect with the melancholly Looks of this desolate Temple, we took our leave of it, and shot directly into the Village; at our first Salutation whereof we chanc'd to pop into a dapper Ale-House, mightily stuft with a huge Hostess, whose Moisture distilling through the Pores of her Body, and being somewhat turn'd through excessive Heat, struck our olfactive Nerves with so great a Sowerness, that we had quite been overcome with this Vessel of Vinegar, had she not too much jogg'd herself by an unhappy Fall, and spilt a great Quantity of her unctuous Liquor. The Shoemaker conjectur'd she had lost about five or six Pounds Avoirdupois, from her Rear, and presently concluded she was in great Danger of hanging all a-one-Side, unless some charitable Person should help her with Thrust of assisting Nose. We had scarce prim'd our Pipes, but in comes a Law-Jobber, accompanied with a Bum-Brusher, or School-Master of the Place, who, after some Time, took Occasion to try their Skill and Breeding at Fistycuffs, but (Thanks to the Stars) without any Danger to their Professions; for they did not so much Aim at the Head, as level their Fury at each others Heels, where their Knowledge was not suppos'd to lie, tho' some there held that they had as much Learning at one End, as they had at t'other.

At this blind Alehouse, I and *Crispin*'s Disciple lay one Night, whence, we sojourn'd together into *Bedfordshire*, till we came to *Dunstable*, a Town builded by King *Henry* I. to bridle the Outrageousness of one *Dun*, a notable Thief, from whom it takes its Name. Here, Mr. Snob having a Mistress, and being almost within the Atmosphere of her Presence, began to wind her, and had a great Tendency to the Place were she was; so that I might as soon expect a Stone to fall beyond the Centre, as that this Gentle-Craftsman should budge further; wherefore, nothing was expected now, but an immediate Divorce from each others Company; but before we parted, he oblig'd me with the Prospect both of her Person and Fortune. As for the first, as soon as I saw it, I had greater Reason to congratulate my Eye-sight than before; for she was blest with the most ravishing Aspect, and a snug Face, most prodigiously grac'd with a dainty fine Nose, fasten'd in the Middle; which was not like some Snouts that look more upon one Cheek, than they do upon the other, but shew'd equal Prospect to both, not at all disobliging the Right, by fleering too much on the Left. And then for her Eyes, they are excellent at twiring, and would (I warrant you) be sure to keep the Nose safe, for one look'd one Way, and the other, another. The Woman had a Mouth too, which was somewhat bigger than that of a Blunderbuss, tho' not twice as big as the capacious Bore of a *Winchester* Quart-pot. This Mouth, she put but to one Use, and that's the same we put ours to, that is, to eat three or four Meals in a Day; for it seems, whereas other Women often use theirs in Prating and Twatling, we perceiv'd, that this sav'd her Mouth, and spake through the Nose. As I have given you the Picture of her Person, so now I'll present you with a Landskip of her Fortune. As for her Lands, that is, Pasture-Ground, and Meadow, we could not discern, but that (like a Spot upon the Globe) they took but little Room upon the Surface of the Earth; and (like the Possessions of *Alcibiades*) were but a little Speck to the World. A little Muck would dung her Fallow; one high Table T—— (to speak in the *Oxford* Dialect) would much enrich it, and an Ear of Corn would go near to sow it: 'Tis like, she had Grass enough for a Couple of

Rabbits. Having surveyed the Paramour, and the Portion of this snivelling Cobler, after a Treble go-down out of a Tin-Pot, a right Line Scrape with Left-Leg, and uncouth Doffing off a bad Bonnet, I return'd his Coblership Thanks for his Society, and solemnly took Leave of my Fellow-Traveller.

After this Departure, I was forc'd to beguile away the Time in the shady Solitude of silent Thoughts, which, before, I spent in the brisker Entertainments of Discourse and Dialogue. At length I came into *Cambridgeshire*, some Parts whereof seem'd to be a little *Arabia* of Sand, enough (as I thought) to supply all the Hour-Glasses in the County; nay, perhaps, and that of Time too, till the last Minute. Arriving at the University of *Cambridge*, I lay at *Jesus* College, in the Garden of which Place, I discover'd among some Ruins, the Snout, and some other Limbs of a murder'd Dial; yet it was not so defac'd, but that I could discover in its Physiognomy, some martyr'd Figures, that were yet legible, and there were some Reliques of Lines, that were not quite obliterated by Time, who, I presume, being vext that it should observe his Motions, had out of Envy and Malice, thus far set his Grinders in it, to deface it. Here, the Students, at *Oxford*, would be as drunk as any Woman, outswear a Life-guard-Man, or Horse-Grenadier; and eat, drink, and lie with any Body. But when I saw whole Shoals of great hulking Fellows, in such ragged Gowns, that our *London* Bunters would scorn to pick 'em up, flocking about the Kitchen-door, some with Basons, some with Porringers, some with Pipkins, some with Pans, some with Chamber-Pots, and some with their very Caps, to beg College Broth; I thought the Scene a very lively Resemblance of poor Lazarus, begging for the Crumbs which fell from the Table of *Dives*.

Hence, I went into *Huntingdonshire*, which is a very proper County for unsuccessful Lovers to live in; for upon the Loss of their Sweethearts, they will here find an Abundance of Willow-Trees, so that they may either wear the Willow green, or hang themselves, which they please; but the latter is reckon'd the best Remedy for slighted Love. Passing through *Godmanchester*, I rambled to *Watford* in *Hartfordshire*, near which Town, formerly stood *Langley-Abbey*, the Birth Place of *Nicholas Breakspear*, who in the Year 1154, being advanc'd to the Papal Dignity, assum'd the Name of *Adrian* IV. and tho' he had been a poor Servant, was so proud, as to excommunicate an Emperor of *Germany*, a *Sicilian* King, and the Senators of *Rome*; for these Popes are sawcy Fellows, when they come to wear triple Crowns, as Kings of Heaven, Earth, and Hell; which last Place, they have enjoy'd by Hereditary Right and Succession, many Ages before the Reign of Pope *Joan*.

Going next into *Essex*, which is as subject to Agues, as the Hundreds of *Drury* is to the Pox, and the whole County much noted for its excellent Calves, but the biggest of that Sort of Cattle are the Inhabitants. I pass'd through *Colchester*, and crossing the County, got into *Staffordshire*, where being inform'd at the City of *Lichfield*, that the Thief-taker-General of *England* first receiv'd his damn'd stinking Breath in that County; I did not care for staying long there, for Fear, the Change of this Air should make me as vile, and double corrupted a —— as himself. In case it should be this Fellow's good Fortune to dance at *Tyburn*, betwixt Heaven and Earth, as being unworthy of either, the Ordinary of *Newgate* may give this Account of him in his dying Speech; how that his Parentage was very obscure and mean;

his Livelihood at first was obtaining Charity from Milk-Maids, and other Country Lasses, by squeezing pretty Ditties out of the Womb of a Bladder, with a Piece of Packthread; and if he should prove so harden'd at the Gallows, as to make no larger Confession of himself, set him down (like *Paul Lorrain*) obstinate. In fine, he had such a bad Character among his own Country-Men, that some said, it was great Pity he had not been hang'd as soon as he was breech'd; whilst others reply'd, that he ought never to die, but be toss'd from D——l to D——l, till there was no Hell left to toss him in any longer.

I soon made the best of my Way into *Shropshire*, where, at a little Town, or rather Village, call'd *Woor*, happen'd a sad Misfortune; for a certain Glass-Case, by Reason of the Rudeness of two lusty Pusses, but whether affrighted at their Catter-wauling, or it being not able to bear them in the Acts of Love, I cannot tell which, but certain it was, it let go its Hold, and after a dismal Manner, came blundering down, attended with the Ruin of several Jiggumbobs, and Jimcracks, as the Ivory Gums of a toothless Comb, a little bottle-breech'd Glass replenish'd with Love Powder; a Brace of blind Needles, that lost their Eyes in the Fall; a double Scut of a Hare ty'd up with a single Packthread; the latter End of an old Broomstick; the Butt End of an old Sugar-Loaf; the true Lovers Knot made in Wire, a square bit of Tin, the Margin of a broad Hat, one Finger-Stall, two Taggs, a Fescue made of Brass Wire, a crack'd Glass with a Club-Foot, the Skin of an Onion stuft with Arsenick, and one Whisker of a bearded Arrow. But as one Misfortune seldom comes alone, so this was attended with another, for a young *Salopian* Lass who was the Proprietor of these Things, took the Accident of them so much to Heart, that she very decently hang'd herself, to the no small Comfort, to be sure, of her Parents, who had six or seven Children, besides this unhappy Daughter, whom nobody could blame for this Piece of Rashness; for is it not a sad Thing to lose so commodious a Place, to lay pretty Things in, and all by the Misdemeanour of two unmannerly Cats? For where could this poor Creature afterwards have laid her Gally-Pots, Gums, and Pomatum? Had these Mousehunters only eas'd Nature there, and then jingerly departed, they had been very excusable, but first to come slily into a Ladies Chamber, and then to squabble and fall out there, and in the Midst of their Quarrel to pursue one another to the Top of a Shelf, and there to renew the Battle again, and to box one another 'till they fell themselves, and demolish'd that very Thing which supported them in their bickering, as the Fool in the Fable saw'd off the Bough he sat on, Oh! this is a very sad Thing indeed, and would make any other young Woman, who had no more Sense then she, hang herself likewise.

But bidding Adieu to the proud *Salopians*, I went into *Cheshire*, where the Towns ending much upon the *Wich*, as *Nantwich, Middlewich, Northwich*; I thought they affected the *Dutch* Way of putting one Name to the End of their Towns, as *Rotterdam, Schiedam, Amsterdam*, and so forth.

In the City of *Chester*, I happened to lie at a Physician's House, whose Pretences to Learning were very great, but by our Conversation, I found him to have more Stomach than Brains, and therefore was more like to have more Consolation in the Kitchin, than in a Study; for there, perhaps he might find a Jobb of Work for his Grinders; whereas he knew not what to do with his Books, unless he should act the

Moth, and eat them. I perceiv'd his Parts to lie more towards the Powderingtub, than his *Pharmacopeia*; for whilst he was busy in the former, he might keep himself alive, but when he read in the latter, he would kill his Patients. We had some roast Beef for Supper; and I commonly found him within an Inch of the Dripping-pan, with an Acre of Bread in his Hand, which he call'd a Sop, and with it, when my Back was turn'd, he usually spung'd up the Dripping, whereby he cheated Sir-Loyn, and robb'd his Knighthood of its due Moisture. Hence, I went into the County of *Northumberland*, where I found *Newcastle*, almost entirely surrounded with Coal Pits, whence seeing Myriads of Men, as black as *Old Nick*, ascending out of the subterranean Shops, upon the Surface of the Earth, I imagin'd them to have been so many *Cyclops* who had been helping *Vulcan* to forge Thunderbolts for *Jupiter*. Not liking the Conversation of these *English* Negroes, I stept over the River *Tine* into the County of *Durham*, where, in the City bearing the same Name, I lay one Night; and next Morning taking my Leave of my Landlady, about half a Mile from the Town, I saw a Church-Yard, where was a whole Herd of Swine a routing, as if they had been turn'd in on Purpose to root up *Christians*, as they are in the Fields in *Italy*, to dig up Turfles. A little Wall lay sculking about this Territory of the dead, which I suppose, was plac'd there as a Bulwark to their Ashes; but it prov'd but a feeble Fence against the Intrusion of the Lambs, who made frequent Capreols into this silent Dormitory: The Mound was rais'd a little, capt with Turf, and environ'd with the Hollowness of a good handsome Ditch; but yet, neither Cap, nor Ditch could keep these Animals from leap-frogging over them, from grazing in a Charnel-House, and from turning a Cœmitery of Shades, and Ghosts into a feeding Pasture of hungry Beasts.

At last, I got into *Yorkshire*, where, beyond *Northallerton*, meeting with a Herdsman, I was almost frighted out of my Wits, for this Fellow was a strange Creature, wonderfully *Goth'd*, and be-*Vandall'd*, even to Barbarity itself. He was really a Clown in grain, an uncultivated Boor, a Beast of the Herd in Humane Shape. I propos'd a Query or two about the Genius of the County; he told me the Soil was cold, and big with Clay, and would doubtless yield a good Harvest of Tobacco-Pipes; and as for the Inhabitants, he said, they were a Pap-Pudding Sort of People, much addicted to that vile Sort of Creature. As he said, I saw a whole Table at a Christening, spread with a Yard of Pudding, and a Balk of Beef, a Ridge at one End and a Furrow at the other; which did so wonderfully work upon the Chaps of the Gossips, and make their Mouths water, that the Godfathers and Godmothers fell furiously to Snouting for some few Morsels; mean while the two ear'd Pitcher, that stood upon the Bench, was Mr. *Prynn'd* in Scuffle, that is, lost a Lug in the Fray; and as I was afterwards inform'd, the Distaff lost a Lock or two of its flaxen Perriwig. The Women of this Country are very coming, and are as great Breeders, as any of our *English Quakers*; and as for the Men, they are naturally born Thieves, being as dextrous Rogues at Horse-Stealing as a Serjeant at the *Poultry*, or *Wood-street-Compter* in selling Minutes dearer than a Watchmaker. But among rational Wonders in a Village, where I say, the most remarkable W o n d e r was an eminent Cot-Quean, a meer Woman in the Habit of a Man, a Kind of *Mol Cut-Purse* Creature, an Epicene Animal of a twisted Gender, who had a Petticoat Soul in a trunk-breech'd Body, and scandaliz'd Virility, by Skill in Housewifery. He spun (the Neighbours said) like a Spider, and made his Wheel giddy by a swift *Vertigo*. He was a learned Craftsman in the making of Diet, a notable Food-Framer, who buffeted Cream, till he frighted it into a Consistence, and then knocking it into Butter, squeez'd it afterwards with Dexterity of Fist. He was also endow'd with the Gift of tossing Pancakes, and had a wonderful Knack at tempering the Materials of a Bag-Pudding, insomuch, that he surpass'd all the Dairy-Maids in the Milk-Pan Accomplishments; and was also excellently well qualify'd for a Meal-Tub Office. Here I tasted of the Hospitality of this fœmasculine Wight, who spread a Jointstool with several Sorts of Viands, which though not very delicate, yet the Variety might attone and make amends for their Meanness. Here was the *Epidermis* of a Hog, the outward Skin, call'd the Sword of Bacon, which was infected with the Jaundies, for it look'd very yellow; next, was the Hull of a Pescod, plunder'd of its Pease, and corn'd with Salt; some broken Fragments of Sheeps Trotters, *St. Laurenc'd* on a Gridiron; the minc'd Spurs of a bootless Cock, a skin'd Quadrant of soft Cheese, well sawc'd with the Butt-ends of forked Scallions; and the mouldy Reversion of an antiquated Loaf, dipt in the Verdure Watercresses Pottage, which afforded me the Refreshment of a pretty Collation: After which I went to Bed, and slept very sound till next Morning. When, getting that Day, into *Newark* upon *Trent, Nottinghamshire*, I was no sooner arriv'd into the Navel of the Town, but I saw such an Assembly of Provision as represented a Market, which was unhappily disturb'd by an unfortunate Accident; for a certain Bull of an uncertain Man, having mistaken his Box, and taken Pepper in the Nose instead of Snuff, and being enrag'd and heated by Virtue of the Spice, took a frisk about the Cross, and empty'd by his Ramble all Stalls and Panniers; so that this brisk Customer made a scrambling kind of Dinner for the whole County; for the Mob, *alias* the civiliz'd Rabble, was riding upon one anothers Backs for Viands and Booty, and was tumbling among the Ruins of Bakers, Butchers, and Costermongers.

Hence I made a Pilgrimage to *Grantham* in *Lincolnshire*, where a little out of Town I over took a Fellow, who began to strike up with his Pipe, and thinking he had but one, he presently perceiv'd it to be multiply'd into an Organ, and wonder'd (with the Bumpkin that pull'd at the Bellows) that he had so much Harmony in him. For you must know hereabouts dwelt a Thing call'd an *Eccho*, who as soon as she heard *Sol, fa*, whip! she improv'd the Melody into Noise and Consort; presently increasing those single Notes into the whole *Gamut*; and most neatly play'd the Wag with the Tail of his Voice, being a very pretty Songster, that sings well by the Ear. But leaving the Piper by himself to solace with the tatling Reverberation of Voice, I proceeded on my Journey into *Rutlandshire*, the least County in *England*, where at *Oakham*, the Shire-Town, is a Custom, that when a Nobleman comes on Horseback within its Precincts, the Inhabitants make him pay the Homage of a Shoe from his Horse, or take Money for it. And so exorbitant is this Custom grown now, that if a Lady, be she as tall as long *Meg* of *Westminster*, or as short as the little Woman, that was carried formerly about the Country in a Box, as fat as the Royal Sovereign the largest first Rate Fire-Ship that sails *Drury-Lane*, and the narrow Seas contiguous to it, or as lank as *Pharaoh*'s lean Kine, they would swear she was a *Flander*'s Mare, and presently take toll from her Foot. This Sharpness hath made most of the *Rutlandshire* People, much addicted to the Vice of Theft; every

Thing sticks to their pitchy Fingers; and they have such an attractive Virtue, that wherever they come, all Things trot after the Magnetism of their Persons. A Fellow squating upon a Criket in a Room I was in, and rising up from his Seat, the Stool on a Sudden (as if tackt to his Backside) immediately march'd after him, to the great Amazement of the Woman of the House, who did not suspect, that his Bum had Hands, or that her Stool so nimbly could have us'd its Legs. Another espying a Cylinder of Bag-Pudding pretty Thick in the Waste, lolling upon the Table, whilst the Hostess turn'd her Back, in the very twinkling of her Head, pocuss'd it into Fob, and so shrouded its Dimensions into a second Bag. Moreover observing a joulter headed Fellow, looking very wishfully at my Head, fearing he had some Design upon what few Brains I had, to furnish his own empty Noddle; I presently paid my Reckoning, and made the best of my Way for *London*; where I was no sooner arriv'd, but perceiving most People murmuring at the great Indulgence then extended to the *Dissenters*, I composed (at the earnest Request of some Friends) the following Lines on Toleration.

Religion! *Now a meer fantastick Name,*
The Heathens *Glory, but the* Christians *Shame;*
A Cloak for Hyprocites, *the Tool of State,*
And, to decoy dull Fools, the Levites Bait;
Thy Lustre *was not tarnish'd in the Time*
When Vice *was ill, and* Virtue *was no Crime?*
When holy Folks from Sin *for Refuge fled,*
And no Dissention *in Opinions bred.*
In the first Infancy *of humane Race,*
The World was overshadowed with Grace;
The very Light of Nature Goodness *taught,*
And humble Vot'ries to the Altar brought;
Where Hecatombs, *no longer doom'd to live,*
Sincere Devotion *did to Heaven give.*
Again, the Jews *were not so very blind,*
But they in Rites *and* Types *cou'd Blessings find;*
Mosaic *Customs, and* Levitic Rules,
Was all the Doctrine of the Rabbins *Schools:*
In mystic Rites, and ceremonial Laws,
With God *and* Angels *they cou'd plead their Cause.*
But now the Temple-Veil *is drawn aside,*
Which did the Truth in Hieroglyphicks hide,
The great Messiah, *by a wond'rous Birth,*
From Heaven *came, to preach to Men on Earth;*
Whose sacred Sermons *shew'd the certain Way,*
How all the World Jehovah *must obey:*
And by his seamless Garment *we may see,*
One only Faith *does please the* Deity.
So Toleration's *but* a Wile, *to draw*
Dissenters *from the* Gospel *and the* Law;

But none by such Indulgence *will be shamm'd,*
But Fools, that will in spite of Fate be d——'d.

THE COMICAL PILGRIM,
OR,
TRAVELS THRO' WALES.

Having had a Suit of Law in Chancery, which was lost thro' my Lawyers Mismanagement, at the Charge of twenty five Pounds out of Pocket, I could not forbear making the following Observations on the Unhappiness of those People who go to Law.

Some are so zealous to ruin one another, that *Westminster-Hall* is every Term made the Place of Destruction. They fasten upon, worry and tear one another; and he that gets the better, generally pays so dear for his Victory that he had better have sat down by the Loss. Not that I would, with the *Socinians*, stretch that Command of our Saviour to his Disciples, to let the Coat go after the Cloak, and make it a Sin against the Gospel, for Christians to go to Law, any farther, than that they should not contend for Trifles. *Christianity* lays no Body open to be abus'd, and impos'd upon, where a regular Remedy may be had. It forbids doing as we would not be done by, and obliges us to bearing and forbearing, rather than to be litigious; but takes away no Body's Property, nor gives so much Countenance to Injustice, as to disarm the oppress'd from recovering their Right. Had going to Law been a Crime in itself, it had never been permitted to the *Jews*. They were allow'd it, and had Courts by divine Appointment erected for the Determination, of what belong'd to every Man. And it is too much for a few singular Dissenters upon a Text, to take upon themselves the putting a Bar to *Christian* Liberty, which in all Ages has been admitted. Nor can we see here that these Precepts of the Sermon upon the Mount, be confin'd as some would have them, to the first Ages only: That what was legal in those Days, it is not the same now. It seems to be from too much Inclination to the World, such Expositions have been set up, that make a Difference in Times and Seasons, as if the Precepts of the Gospel were not always of the same Obligation; and we could excuse ourselves in the Contempt of them, because we are not the Persons they were immediately deliver'd to.

Tho' the litigious Humour of some Men richly deserve a chargeable Remedy, there is yet a Commiseration due sometimes to their Antagonist. A Man may, whether he will or not, be engag'd in these bloody Conflicts at the Suit of his Neighbour's Pride or Malice. And since the most peaceable Temper may be oblig'd to complain of Oppression, or answer the Charge of Picque and Revenge; 'tis Pity but Justice were to be obtain'd at a cheaper Rate, and a slight Wound may be cur'd without Amputation, which nothing but a Gangrene can justify. We could wish the Law were less chargeable; that seeking Right were not as bad as suffering Wrong: That the Avenues to Justice were not to be set with Robbers, that a Man must lose one Purse to recover another, and be stript into the Bargain. *Justice* (we are told) should be blind, and so we think she is, when she can't see the exorbitant Fees of her Attendants. When to be let in and let out, costs so much Oppression, nothing could have been severer. When the Man that's summon'd to answer in a litigious Suit, must go thro' so many Toils, and be so often spung'd in his Passage, he might as well have pass'd for Guilty, as pleaded Innocence: Like the Christians in *Turkey*, who pay double Taxes for their Religion, and hire infidel Moderation to connive at their Patriarch's Jurisdiction. Why these Imposts were laid upon the Road to Justice, we never could understand. How that can be made out, we are much at a Loss. Which of the liberal Arts or Sciences thrives upon the Fees of Door-Keepers? Is copying and Abbreviation so essential a Point to Learning, a Nation could not have maintain'd a Character without it? Are so many Lines a Sheet, and so many Words in a Line, so Mathematical a Substraction of ones Money, that the Credit of the Nation must rise in Proportion to the Losses of the poor Meagre, wasted *Culprit*? We are told too 'tis upon a politick Account, to prevent Contention: That the more difficult is the Way to Justice, the more People are inclin'd to be quiet. If the Courts were open to every Grievance, there would be Complaints without End. A Hog could not go thro' a Stone Yard, but the Law must be rais'd against the Trespasser. A Man could not be an Hour without a *Subpœna* or Attachment, if there was Room for every Body's Impertinence. 'Twould prevent Contention as effectually, if the Person in Fault were punish'd; if paying sufficient Cost to the Adversary or Fine, were inflicted by the Court upon a litigious Plaintiff, or roguish Defendant.

As the Cause stands, the Law is a Weapon for the Proud, and revengeful. These may be in the Right, at least have their Revenge, if their Purse be the longest. So chargeable have been the Methods of bringing Oppressors to Account, so expensive the Armour to defend the Innocent, that one may think the first Loss had been the best, and the other wish he had let the Coat go to him that had taken away the Cloak. There's a Revolution indeed of Estates, and where the Law has broke one Family, it has rais'd another. If the Desolation the Law has made, were recorded, and the Ensigns of the Orphans and Widows were hung up, whose forlorn Relations have been press'd into the Service, there would be no Room for those brought from the *Danube* and *Ramellies*. 'Tis true, much may be said in Favour of a mistaken Client, in Excuse of Ignorance, Passion, and the like: But where a Man engages in a Cause palpably litigious and unjust, he becomes a Party to the Injustice, and deserves at least equal Punishment with him he appears for. *Thou sawest a Thief, and consentedst unto him,* is chargeable upon the Pleader, as a Person concern'd. Should these Maintainers of Learning be mercenary, and like Sergeants at the *Compter*, gape at every Retainer? Should they have an Indulgence to cross-bite an Evidence, to abuse the Adversary, and rip up the Misfortunes of his Family, and belch a few Witticisms instead of Arguments? How shall the World maintain Reverence to their Opinion? How shall we take them for the Guides of Conscience, set aside the receiv'd Interpretation of the Law, and believe them when they say, *The Case is alter'd*? I shall say no more upon this Point, but only use these Words of our Saviour, *Woe unto you also, ye Lawyers: For ye lade Men with Burdens grievous to be born, and ye yourselves touch not the Burdens with one of your Fingers. Wo unto you Lawyers: For ye have taken away the Key of Knowledge: Ye enter'd not in yourselves, and they that were entring in, ye hindred.*

Being quite surfeited with seeing the Legerdemain, or *hocus pocus* Tricks of Madam *Astræa*, *alias* Justice, the Day after *Trinity-Term* being, drest with *Aurora*, nay before she had put on her *Indian* Gown, I set out with the Sun in order to take a Pilgrimage into *Wales*, who bearing me Company but little while, withdrew into an Appartment behind a Cloud, at whose Absence, the Heavens frowning and contracting their Brows, did presently fall a crying, and wept such plentiful Showers of Tears that they moistned my Skin with the Deluge of their Grief. At the End of 8 or 9 Days, I reach'd *Wales*, which is the most monstrous Limb in the whole Body of Geography; for 'tis generally reported to be without a Middle, or if it hath a Navel, it is yet a *Terra incognita*; for I never could find that ever any Man dwelt there, the Natives confessing themselves only Borderers. Surely the Reason why they do so much affect the Circumference of their Country, and abominate the Centre, is, because they are asham'd of the Dominion; and indeed, 'tis a Sign they have but a little Kindness for their Nation, who (like unnatural Sons) run from their Mother their Country, and when out of her Embraces, never return again. A *Welshman*, when once abroad, hath no more Tendency Home, than a Stone an Inclination to fall upward: He will trot o'er the Globe, and rather endure the Affliction of any Exile, than the cruel Punishment of being banish'd Home; if he is once on this Side *Dee*, neither Hunger, nor Husks, nor any Kind of Hardship shall drive him on the other.

No sooner had I set my Feet upon *Welsh* Turf, but in a little Time I found the Country was tuckt in on all Sides with the Sea, except on the East, on which Part it was ditch'd in from *England* by that notable Delver, King *Offa*, King of the *Mercians*: Over this Dike, if any *Welshman* chance to skip with his Sword by his Side, by King *Harold*'s Law, he was to lose a Branch of his Body, *i. e.* his right Arm was lopt off by the King's Officers. Some think it had its Name from its Godfather *Idwallo*, Son to *Cadwallader*, who with a small Crew of *Britons*, at the Arrival of the *Saxons*, hid themselves in this Corner. Others suppose them to be the Spawn of the *Gauls*, from whom they seem to be but a few *Aps* remov'd; *ap Galloys, ap Gauls, ap Wallois, ap Wales.*

As for the Inhabitants, they are a pretty Sort of Creatures, which when I saw, I was so far from stroaking them with the Palms of Love, that I was almost ready to buffet them with the Fist of Indignation. They are a rude People, and want much Instruction. Not one *Welshman* is sharp, unless his Mother happens to pour Vinegar into his Ear, when young. When I consider the Soil from whence they sprang, and the Desarts, and Mountains wherein they wander, I cannot but think, that greater Pains should be taken in cultivating and manuring, in disciplining, and taming them, in Regard 'tis harder for a Bearward to teach Civility to the Beasts of *Africk*, than those who come from a more mannerly Country. I have been inform'd that they were dug from a Quarry, and that they dwell in a stony Land; so that if we compare this Kingdom to a Man, as some do *Italy* to a Man's Leg, they inhabit the very Testicles of the Nation. And I pray what are those but the vilest of Creatures that breed as well in the Privities of the greater *British* World, as those that are hatcht in the *Pudenda* of the lesser? But whether *Welshmen* are the *Aborigines* of their Country, as Crab-Lice are the *Autocthones* of theirs, and proceed only (like them) from the Excrements of their Soil, I shall not here dispute. They are of a boorish Behaviour, of a savage Physiognomy; the Shabbiness of their Bodies, and the Baoticalness of their Souls, and that, which cannot any otherwise be exprest, the *Welchness* of both, will fright a Man as fast from them, as the Odness of their Persons invites one to behold them. Some of them are such rude and indigested Lumps, so far from being Men, that they can scarce be advanc'd into living Creatures; nay they are such unmanageable Materials, that they can scarce be hewn into the Shape of Blocks; much Labour and Art is requir'd therefore to make them Statues.

The whole Nation (like a *German* Family) is of one Quality; for as every Lord's Son is a Lord in *Germany*, so every one is crown'd with the Title of Gentleman here; so that hur Country is a good Pasture for an Herald to bite in. In their Travels they care not much that their Horses should drink with a Toast, as appears by the which a *Shinkin* discover'd, whom his quaffing Beast had pitch-pol'd into a River. Udsplutter-a-nails quoth he in great Fury, what cannot hur drink without a Toast? He took it much in dudgeon, that the Jade should be so bold as to make a Sop of his Master.

The Materials of his Apparel are usually a well shagg'd Freeze, so that we cannot call it sleepy, being fleec'd with a Nap like any Sheep-Skin: It affords excellent Harbour to the Vermin of his Body, which whether it be stockt with Store of Joicements of them, he commonly signifies by the Symbol of a Shrug. The Perfection of a *Welshman*'s Equipage, the Cream (as it were) of his Accoutrements, and that which compleats ever his most festival Attire, is (as the Story goes) an old Sword of hur nown breeding, which hur hath brought up from a Tagger: And this he can brandish with much Valour against the tremenduous on-set of dragooning Bees; a kind of Enemy which the Taffy is much afraid of, in Regard he is always arm'd with a Pike in's Reer, which once upon a Time fastening in his Forehead, broach'd such a Pore in his Physiognomy, that he could never endure those hum-buzzing Gentlemen (as he calls them) in yellow Doublets.

The Country is mountainous, and yields pretty Handsome clambering for Goats, and hath Variety of Precipice to break ones Neck; which a Man may sooner do than fill his Belly, the Soil being barren, and an excellent Place to breed a Famine in. It is reported of *Campania*, that it was the most noble Region in the World, the Air pleasant, the Soil fertil, the Theatre of *Bacchus* and *Ceres*, where they were at fisty-cuffs for the Preheminence: But I perceiv'd no such Scuffle in *Wales*; for those Deities are so far from fighting there, that I could not discern they were so much as ever there; there being scarce Water and Oatmeal to give a Man Being. I could not expect *Egypt* and the *Canaries* Buts and Granaries to give me a well Being: There is no *Canaan* to be found in a Desart. As for the Diet of a *Briton*, a good Mess of Flummery, and a Pair of Eggs, he rejoyces at, as a Feast, especially if he may close his Stomach with toasted Cheese, for a Morsel of which he hath a great Kindness. You may see him pictur'd sometimes with that Crevice in his Head call'd a Mouth, charg'd at both Corners with a Cresent of Cheese, and himself a Cock-Horse on a red Herring, and his Hat adorn'd with a Plume of Leeks: Good edible Equipage! Which when hunger pinches, he makes bold to nibble; he first eats his Cheese and his Leeks together, and for second Course he devours his Horse. But he never much cared for a Sop, since once upon a Time it drank up all his Drink, and would not club to pay his Shot.

The *Cambro-Britons* are great Admirers of heroick Actions, and much Honour the Memory of famous Atchievements; insomuch, that rather than a dead-doing Man shall perish in Oblivion, they will eternize his Memory by the Monument of a Straw, or some such inconsiderable Trifle; as appears by the famous Example of that Saint of their Country, Bishop *David*, who being a pert Fighter, and having soundly basted and swadled their Foes, is at this Day consecrated to Posterity by the Trophy of a Leek; and smells as rank of Renown from that vegetable Preservative that embalms his Fame, as they do of a Scallion that carry it about for his Glory. Their Hats are set with this anniversary Badge, and Emblem of Honour and Triumph, on the first of *March*, which Day hath been christen'd by his Name, and being dubb'd an Holyday, hath worn yearly a black Livery in the Almanack.

Nevertheless, the *Welchmen* being cursedly thick-scull'd, they are so far from being Plotters, that they swear they will never fight for any King upon Earth, but the Prince of *Wales*; because there can be no true Royal Blood running in the Veins of any great Man, but what borrows his Title from their Country, let him be born where he will: And considering what wicked plotting Times we now live in, no Body can blame them for their Cautiousness of being hang'd; for tho' it is a Death natural to them, yet they say, sleeping in a whole Skin is best. Not that they value hanging, but only they abhor the Death, unless the Office is perform'd a by a *Welch* Hangman, instead of an *English* one.

They are much inclin'd to Choler, for hur *Welch* Plood is soon mov'd, and then hur stamp and stare, and scrat hur Pole, and vent hur Fury in Ud-splutter-a-nails, and will fight for hur Life in Battle at fisty-cuffs. They are polite in nothing but Faction and Sedition, for there are high and low Church Parties among them too, which occasions much Contention and Quarrels.

The Musick a *Welchman* plays upon, is a Tool stiled an Harp, with which, when Sustenance fails him, he strikes up for a Morsel, and so lives by Sounds, and (Camelion like) hath Alimony from Air. He serenades Victuals in every Village, as the pide Piper did Rats at *Hamel*, and he allures Luncheons after him, as much as the other did Vermin: Here a Nob of Bacon wags after him, for one Strain; and there a Crust follows him, as the Reward of another; one hits him in the Mouth with the Payment of Pottage, another pops him in the Pocket with the Gratuity of a Carrot; all which Variety of Fragments is the most ample Income, and wonderful Revenue of his Skill in Musick. His usual Admirers are Country Milk-Maids, whom Vibration of String doth move and stir into Jigg and Measure; and whom Breeze of Instrument (like those in Tail) do chase and tickle into Dance and Caper.

I could not perceive that the *Welch* were guilty of much Learning, which made a Man skill'd in Orthography admir'd as a Sophy; and a Writer of his Name, to be term'd a Rabbi. As for the Loves of the *Britons*, the Intrigues of their Amours are not a little remarkable, they being very pretty Animals when disguis'd with that Passion: They are Tinder to such Flames, being quickly set on fire, even by the least Spark, which when it hath catch'd the Match of their Souls (for they have Brimstone in them as well as in their Bodies) they are presently kindled into Transport and Extasy; and these model them into the Shapes of a thousand Anticks, and make them shew more Tricks than old *Preston*'s Bears. Sometimes they are shaking the Globules of their Noddles, and sometimes dancing some Geometry with the Figures of their Feet; now they smite with Clapper of Fist their troubled Breasts, and anon sound out some Knels of dismal Groans; being variously affected as the Weather is in their *Clorinda*'s Faces; if Aspect be clear, then is *Taffy* serene; if brow be cloudy, then is *Morgan* Showry. Whilst I was in this Country, I heard of a *Welchman* that went a wooing with a Gun upon his Shoulder, being resolv'd (it seems) if Love be a Warfare, not to enter unarm'd into the Camp of *Venus*; still as his coy *Daphne* shifted from his Presence, he march'd musketeering about the Room, and most fiercely pursu'd her, till at last in the brisk Encounter of a close Embrace, this warlike Instrument took an Occasion somewhat unmannerly to go off, and blunderbuss'd the Mistress on her Breech on one Side of the House, and poor *Taffy* on his Nose on the other; so that being much dismay'd at this unhappy Accident, one scrabled one Way, and the other another, to the utter spilling of a Mess of Love, and total Separation of a Pair of Lovers for ever.

They are pretty devout in their Worship, tho' the Exercise of Religion is somewhat scarce, and have a pretty glowing Zeal, tho' their Churches are few, and at a great Distance. 'Tis almost incredible how far they are fain to trudge for a little Homily; which when they have expected, have been mump'd with a Sermon ten Times worse. For on such raw-bone Livings, there cannot be expected very plump Parts. The ordinary Revenue of a spiritual Preferment may possibly be about five Marks *per Annum*; a Bay of Watling for a Dwelling, endow'd with no more Glebe than just what it stands upon, only perhaps it may be how-stall'd with as much Ground as may hold a Sty for the Pig, and a Roost for the Pullen. These divine Cottages are usually situated some Leagues from the Temple, so that the Holy Man with Crab-Tree Truncheon sets out with the Sun, and stretches his Legs with a good handsome Walk, before he arrives at the Pulpit to stretch his Lungs, and wears out much of his Soles before he can reach his Stall to mend their Souls, Their Houses of Prayer are generally thatcht Tabernacles, which are wainscoted towards the East with little Desks, like Pounds, where *Levite* imprison'd for about half an Hour, fodders the poor *Taffies* with some *melancholy* Tear-fetching Story about a grim Fellow call'd Death, who ambles Folks on his Back into another World; a Thing which he heard from the oracular Gums of his edentulous old Granum, as she sate on the Settle in the Chimney-Corner. Some of the most reverend Rectors are dignify'd with a Stipend of six Pounds a Year, besides the Perquisities of a Drum and Fiddle; which well manag'd on a Holiday, make up a very pretty Thing. Others have an Augmentation of a Bull or a Bear, which being solemnly baited about twice in a Quarter, do pick pretty comfortable Tyth from the Spectators Pockets, and makes the poor Parson's Purse to smile and mantle.

As far as I could perceive, the *Welch* People love Holiday Fingers, and care not much for encumbring them with that Inconvenience call'd Work. They can (Shepherd like) loll upon a Crook pretty handsomely in the Field, and can discharge a Superintendency over the Goats. They are most accomplish'd Drovers, to which laudable Function they are so naturally prone, that they are apt to drive sometimes more than their own. They are much addicted to the Sin of Nastiness, wallowing in Filthiness like so many Swine; so that the whole Nation seems but a general Sty. The meaner Sort of Women are generally such draggle Tails, that the Cattle in their Bosoms are quag-mir'd in the Filth of their well-gleb'd Attire; so that the frisking Fleas are so far from *Levalto*'s, that I was verily persuaded they can scarce pull out *Proboscis*, and their Feet from the Bogs. The Tenements they live in are suitable to the Guests that possess them; for as these seem to be Dirt moulded into Men, so those are the same Matter kneaded into Houses; they are usually very humble Cottages, and low in Stature, so that a Man may ride upon the Ridge, and yet have his Legs hang in the Diet. I was not so vain as to expect very splendid Furniture in such contemptible Huts; but I soon perceiv'd what Utensils were most necessary, a Dish-Clout and a Besom, and such cleansing Implements are very proper to correct the Filthiness of their Mansions. I found no Apartments in these their Habitations, every Edifice being a *Noah*'s Ark, where a promiscuous Family, a miscellaneous Heap of all Kind of Creatures did converse together in one Room; the Pigs and the Pullen, and other Brutes either truckling under, or lying at the Bed's-Feet of the little more refin'd, yet their Brother Animals.

But that which I admir'd most of all amongst them, was the Virginity of their Language, not deflowerd by the Mixture of any other Dialect. The Purity of the *Latin* was debauch'd by the *Vandals*, and hunn'd into Corruption by that barbarous People; but the Sincerity of the *British* Tongue remains inviolable. 'Tis a Tongue (it seems) not made for every Mouth, as appears by an *English* Gentleman one Day in my Company, who having got a *Welsh* Polysyllable into his Throat, was almost choak'd with Consonants, had I not, by clapping him on the Back, made him disgorge a Guttural or two, and so sav'd him. Whether the *Welsh* Tongue be a Splinter of that universal one that was shatter'd at *Babel*, I have some Reason to doubt, in Regard 'tis unlike the Dialects that were crumbled there. However, 'tis now cashir'd out of Gentlemen's Houses, there being scarcely to be heard even one single *Welsh* Tone in many Families; for their Children are instructed in the *Anglican* Idiom, and their Schools are pædagogu'd with Professors of the same; so that (if the Stars prove lucky) there may be some glimmering Hopes that the *British* Tongue may be quite extinct, and may be *English'd* out of *Wales*, as *Latin* was barbarously *Goth'd* out of *Italy*.

But in fine, being quite out of Conceit with the short Commons I met with in this Mountainous Country, which was much inferiour to the delicious Dainties of Water-Gruel, Bread and Butter, and Small Beer, allow'd to the poor Lunaticks of *Bedlam*, after they come to pig in Straw, and have their Heads shav'd as an Introduction to Phlebotomy, three or four Times a Week, I e'en bade adieu to the miserable *Taffies*, and made the best of my Way to *England* again, to recover that Flesh in a plentiful Nation, which I had lost in a Land of meer Poverty and Famine.

THE COMICAL PILGRIM'S PILGRIMAGE
INTO SCOTLAND.

eing returned out of *Wales* into *England* again, I was no sooner got into *London*, but thro' an avaricious Temper, I soon began to haunt most of the Gaming-Houses in Town, which Day and Night were as well cram'd as the Groom-Porter's Table. In these Schools of inevitable Ruin and Destruction, I lost a great deal of Money, and when too late to recover it, I began seriously to reflect with my-self, that let a Man be ever such a good Gamester at Cards or Dice, yet so many Sharpers were always flocking about him, that they would drain his Pockets in spite of all the greatest Favours of Fortune; or else how could these Gaming-Houses clear sometimes 100 Pounds, but never less than 50 or 60 Pounds a Night, besides paying Salaries to the several Officers depending solely on them? For there *Commissioners* are maintain'd by whom the Weeks Accompt is Audited, *viz. Directors*, who Superintend the Room. *Operators*, or Dealers at Faro. *Croupees*, to watch the Cards, and gather the Money for the Bank. *Puffs*, who have Money given them to play, in order to decoy others. *Clerks*, who are Checks upon the Puffs, to see that they sink none of that Money. *Squibs*, who are Puffs of a lower Rank, having half their Salary; *Flashes*, who sit by to Swear how often they have stript the Bank; *Dunners*, or Waiters; *Attornies*, or Sollicitors; *Captains*, who are to Fight any Men that are Peevish, or out of Humour at the loss of their Money; *Porters*, who at most of the Gaming-Houses are Soldiers; *Ushers*, who take care that the Porters at the Door suffer none to come in but those they know; and *Runners*, to get Intelligence of all the Meetings of the Justices of the Peace, and when the Constables go upon the Search: Besides giving half a Guinea to any Link-Boy, Coach-man, Chairman, Drawer, or other Person, who gives Notice of the Constables being upon the Search.

Now to break myself from this bewitched Gaming, I bid adieu to Hazard, Back-gammon, Tick-tack, l'Ombre, Picquet, Cribbidge, and Basset, and was resolved to take a Pilgrimage into *Scotland*, where I found the Inhabitants addicted to no sort of Game but *One and Thirty*, at which they are as dextrous as a Milk-Maid at Dancing on *May-Day*, with one Foot upon the Ground, and t'other never off; for from *Fergus* their first King down to *Charles* the First, whom they Sold for a Sacrifice to Stratocracy or Army Power, they had Murder'd no less than Thirty One of their Sovereigns, which is just the Game at Regicide: Hereupon to call them Traytors is a Favour, for they will hatch Treason as soon as they do *Chickens* at *Grand-Cairo*, by the Adoption of an Oven; but now the *Scots* are bound to their good Behaviour, by a Union, they ought to be as Circumspect in their Loyalty, as the Ambassador that Beds a Queen, with the nice Caution of a Sword between them.

It is said that *Scota* the Daughter of *Pharaoh* King of *Egypt*, who was Drown'd in the *Red-Sea*, gave Name to *Scotland*, when she went thither, and betwixt which People and the valiant *English*, a Quarrel continued longer than ever did any between any other two Nations in the World, for they have most obstinately contended (like *Rome* and *Carthage*) for Empire above 2000 Years; which is the most tenacious Suit that ever depended between any two People in the Court of *Mars*. Since the *Norman* Invasion, there have been 30 pitcht Battles betwixt us and them; of which the *English* have obtain'd of the *Scots* at least four for one, and those of greatest Consequence. The South Part of *Great-Britain* being Champian, hath been sometimes in its Borders harrass'd, and laid wast by the *Scots*, never possess'd, but their Country, defended by inaccessible Hills, and by two invincible Enemies, Hunger and Cold, hath been wholly reduc'd by the *English*, who have Slain four *Scotch* Kings, and took two Prisoners; whereas they have never Slain nor took Prisoner one *English* King, to whom the Kings of *Scotland* were Homagers for a long Time.

Those *Scots*, who dwell by the Sea, dung their Land with the Weeds which it casts on the Shore; and all Women throughout the Country in Writing use their Maiden Names after Marriage. About the High and Solitary Hills of *Genap* I saw good Store of Magpyes and Goats; but few Hogs, to whose Flesh they bear as utter an Aversion as the *Jews*; and among all their Flocks of Sheep, where you'll see one White, there's ten Black, so that you may soon know a *Scotchman* from a black Sheep. The farther I Travell'd, I observ'd Geese were not over plentiful; Parsnips very scarce; Venison not to be had for want of Deer; Boys Knitted, and Men, Women, and Children went bare-legg'd.

As for their Coyn, the most remarkable of their Coyning is a *Baubee*, which is the value of our Half-penny, bearing the royal Effigy on one side, and on the Reverse the Thistle and Crown, with this Motto, *Nemo me impune lacessit*. In the Kirk-Yard at *Girvan* are several Carv'd Grave-stones; and at the Kirk-Door in this Town are fasten'd Jogs or Brad-Irons to Chains three or four Feet long; which are put round Persons Necks, who Swear, get Drunk, or break the Sabbath. Thus by countenancing Religion in allowing their Pastors to have an Authority over Misdemeanors, it is that the tumultuary *Scottish* Institution has gain'd Ground, and insinuated itself into popular Credit and Esteem: For on every *Sunday*, when the Office of the Day is over, they have a Kirk-Sessions, wherein the Minister, with a Number of his Congregation Elected to that end, is Authoriz'd to meet and take Cognizance, and to punish all Offenders the foregoing Week. So some such Authority, and a few more insulting Priviledges, seem to be some of those *Desiderata*'s aim'd at by our pretended Reformers of Manners in *England*, to make up their Temporal Advantages, under a specious show of designing to restore the more Primitive and *Christian* Discipline. But I hope this Age will never experience what it is to come under the Pharisaical Constitution of such pious Cheats. Nevertheless, since Knowledge without Virtue has abus'd the World with too much Impiety, I applaud that one Thing of the reforming Societies in *England*, in putting poor

Children out to Trades; for of what Use is Learning (any farther than Reading and Writing) to ordinary Vocations? Whatsoever exceeds, is Useless, and makes them Pragmatical: Moreover, as it is not their Happiness to obtain Advantages of a more liberal or academical Education, it will much more commend the Goodness of their small Breeding, that they have learnt to speak Truth rather than *Latin*, which the Masters of our Parish Schools understand not; and that they are more knowing and exact in the Rules of Justice (a transcendent Quality unknown to some of their Benefactors) than the Distinction of Languages.

In my Journey not far from the Town of *Ayre*, many Sales are to be taken on the Sea-Coasts; but on the Land not many Pidgeons, nor great Store of wild Ducks: However, the Country is well stockt with other sort of Foul, as foul Plates, foul Dishes, foul Trenchers, foul Knives, foul Forks, foul Napkins, and by Heavens foul ever thing else, even to their very Women, who you'll see standing on a *Saturday* by a lolling Wash-block, which is a Wooden kind of Anvil, where the She-*Vulcans* are hammering out with Battledore, or else with their Feet in a washing *Tub*, the Filth of Linnen, whose unctious Distillations are the *Nile* that water'd the little *Egypt* of their adjacent Gardens. Staring very earnestly with all the Eyes that I had, as if looking thro' a Perspective Glass, I perceiv'd every *Scotchman*'s Face usually bubbled into Bubbles and Pustulees, besides the natural Hout-goust of Body that breath'd from Oatmeal, which made him send forth an Artificial Smell, which you might wind as far as the extream Unction of 20 *Romish* Funerals, only the Scent is not so Sweet; besides the bonny *Scot* smells as rankly of the single Stink of Brimstone, as a Goldfinder, *alias*, Tom-Turd-Man of a Medley; for a scurvey Disease, commonly call'd the Scrubbado, otherwise the Itch, makes frequently an Inroad into his Person, and invades his Body; so that he is forced to choak his Enemy by Stink of Sulphur. 'Tis a Creeping Distemper, whose Progress is checkt by Mortification, so that when he leaves off his Shirt, that is, when it leaves him, and can hang on no longer, it is excellent Furniture for a Tinder-Box, as virtually containing in it both Match and Tinder.

The common People wear Plads and Bonnets, which is a great Fashion in this Country, where the Postman goes a Foot; and poor Folks eat the Stalks of raw Kale. The Elders of the Kirks on *Saturday* night duly haunt the Ale-houses, which they call Changes, to turn out People to prepare themselves for the *Sabbath*; and Women here ride astride, without any Danger. The Kirks or Places of Worship have all one Bell, rung by an Iron Chain; but put at either End of the House of Prayer, without any Distinction of East or West, so that Travellers must not look upon their diminutive Steeples for the Guide of a true Course to the Compass.

At the University of *Glascow*, which like their other poor Universities has but one College, I saw no other Learning but the insipid Collegians wearing red hanging-sleev'd Gowns; and the Cathedral here was built by one Mr. *Mongou*, I can't call him Saint, because he was the Son of a Whore begot by a *Danish* Prince on a *Scotch* King's Daughter. Because our main or chief Gallows in *England*, call'd *Tyburn*, hath three Beams, and which is famous for stocking the *Romish* Calendar for roguish Saints, the *Scotch* to exceed us will have four Beams on their hanging Places, made in the manner of a *Turn-Stile*; having on each Beam an Iron Hook, on which the Malefactor is to be expos'd in a pendent Posture betwixt Heaven and Earth, as being unworthy of either. The Men for the most part wear Stockings made of Plad-Stuff; and their Quarters are *Candlemas-Day, May-Day, Lammas-Day*, and *All-hallow Tide*, which are as welcome to their Landlords as our Quarter-Days are among us.

Bad Cooks are every where in this Nation, because they have seldom any Victuals to dress; and the Childrens Cradles here made of old Wainscot without Heads to them. The *Scots* have several old Ways to distinguish themselves from *Christians*, for their Chimes always ring before the Clock strikes; instead of Candles they burn in most Places the Shavings of Fir dipt in Tallow; their Spoons are generally made of Horn quite circular or round, about 3 Inches Diameter, with the Length of the Handle suitable to its Circumference, which Largeness (I suppose) they take from the old Proverb, *He must have a long Spoon that eats with the Devil*; and those People that can but fill their Bellies with thin Bannock, Sourings, or Bruis, which last sort of Food is only raw Oatmeal put into Water when it's warm, and thought by them a great deal better than to dine with Duke *Humphrey*. Hemp and Flax for Linnen are the Staple Commodities of this Nation; but the *Scots* bear a mortal Hatred to the former, because by the Production thereof, a great many of 'em come to an untimely End.

When I came into the City of *Edinburgh*, which is the Capital of the Kingdom, I thought I was got into *West-Smithfield*, for such a Place for Nastiness was not to be found upon Earth, for as the latter was but fill'd with Beasts Dung, the other was more nasty than a common Jakes or Inns-of-Court House of Office, for having a Dung-Tub at the Head of every Pair of Stairs in their Houses, which are 14 or 15 low Stories high, they are emptied a-nights on Peoples Heads without any respect of Persons, so that till 8 or 9 o' th' Clock in the Morning, the whole City, which may be a Mile in Length, is scented with the excellent Perfume of *Scotch* Civit Cats; and all the Woman here look as ugly as the *Four of Clubs*, which some call *Wibling*'s Witch, from one *James Wibling*, who in the Reign of King *James* the First grew rich by private Gaming, and was commonly observ'd to have this Card in his Hand, so that he never lost a Game but when he mist it.

All the *Scots* are generally as great Enemies to Gentility and nice Dressing, as *Diogenes* the morose *Cynic* was to *Plato*, because of his courtly Compliance with the World; and to be honest would be as great a Mortification to them as *Lent* to a poor Player. They'll sit as lovingly about Oaten Cakes and Butter, as a Parcel of Tarpaulins round a Platter of Burgue; and they love Hunger and Ease, as well as a Lawyer does *Term-Time*. Tho' they hate the solemn Festival of *Christmas*, and other Holy-days, yet they pay some Veneration to St. *Andrew*; and will be as Drunk on the *30th* of *November*, as any Shoemaker once a Year to the Remembrance of *Crispin*. They hold Fairs in many Places, at which is much Mobbing, Whoring and Drunkenness as at our *Shirking-Fair* by *Tyburn*: And Mrs. *Cicilia*, they say, is no Saint, but a common Strumpet bred up at a Three-penny Hop in *London*. I never saw the Sign of the *Brats-Tumbler* any where, which makes me believe every *Scotch* Woman brings her Urchins into the World, without the Assistance of Madam *Grope*, to save Charges; on a *Sunday* Morning the *Scots* will run 4 or 5 Miles to a Conventicle; and in the Afternoon to the Mountains to louse themselves.

It is suppos'd by some, that *Scotland* is the Land of *Nod*, to which *Cain* was exil'd a Vagabond for the Murther of his Brother *Abel*; and truly in my Opinion the Supposition may be Very probable, for *Cain*'s being an Inhabitant there, the Ground hath been curst ever since, for it is a most barren Place to this very Day. Had grazing *Nebuchadnezzar* been here, he would have found but bad Pasture; and *Judas* as much plagu'd for a Tree to hang himself on. Bag-Pipes they esteem before Organs; there's as much Hypocrisy in their Pantile-Houses as Irreligion in a *Jews* Synagogue; and the Dog-Days are not so warm here as in more Southerly Climates, but their Bitches Nights every where are too hot with a Vengeance. Here is every Day an Autumn among the Women; for, for a Noggin of Brandy they will fall as thick on their Backs as the Leaves in St. *James*'s Park do in *September*; and Law and Equity are as great Strangers to the *Scots*, as Honesty to the Justice of Peace that's lately run from *Clare-Court* to the *Mint*, and who (when in Commission) was fitter to sit on a Butcher's Block, as his Father did before him, than in a Magistrate's Chair.

The Castle at *Edinburgh* is reckon'd as impregnable as a *Scotchman*'s sear'd Conscience; and their Capital contains but one Broad Street, by which is an University containing one College of Scholars poor both in Purse and Head. Here are no Carts, but sliding Cars; and the highest Number I ever saw on their Hackney Coaches exceeded not 29. The *Scots* reckon their Children spurious if they have not the Itch; and there's as much Whoring every Day, as at *Bartholomew* or *Southwark* Fair. They Bury the Dead at Noon, to save the Charge of Torches; and as here are no Linkmen, only Boys and Girls light Passengers with Candles in Paper Lanthorns all about Town for a Baubee. Most of the People are generally of the Religion with them who marry without a Ring, Christen without the Cross, and Die without Baptism. Their Pastors, who are of the true Stamp of *Geneva*, endeavour by long extemporary Prayers and tedious Graces, to save the poor Souls of those Mountaineers; but yet their Hypocrisie Damns more than ever *Sampson* Slew, and with the same Weapon too, *the Jaw Bone of an Ass*. The *Presbyterian* Government is uppermost here; which Religion being a good quiet Subject, I could not forbear setting forth the Piety of a *Scotch Presbyterian*, in the following Lines.

> CHRISTIANS, *behold a most pernicious sight,*
> *Which worse than Hell wou'd dying Martyrs fright!*
> *Such Monsters* Africk *never did produce;*
> *Nor* Lucifer, *when all his Imps broke loose,*
> *To win, by force of Arms, celestial Sway,*
> *But, unsuccessful, lost the fatal Day:*
> *And if its Name by any shou'd be ask'd,*
> *It is a* Presbyterian *unmask'd.*
> *His Eyes at Vice look sad, and full of Woe,*
> *Yet Heart and Tongue together never go;*
> *His Words in Conventicles virtuous be,*
> *But nauseous, when at Home, to Modesty.*
> *To seem Dovout, he hates all common Whores,*

But those which Ply in Private much Adores.
He trembles when a first Rate Oath he hears;
But Perjury his Int'rest seldom fears.
In solemn Leagues and Covenants he takes
Delight; but greater in the Vows he breaks:
And as informing is his darling Trade,
He is a godly Man in Masquerade.
In fine, he's Born, he Lives, and Dies in Sin;
A Saint without, and Devil all within:
Nay, as his Sanctity's a pious Fraud,
Which none but Knaves and Villains can applaud,
He is all Hypocrite, and what is worse!
The Scorn of Men, and God's eternal Curse.

A *Scotchman's* Tongue runs high Fullams, there is a Cheat in his Idiom; for the Sense ebbs from the bold Expression, like the Citizen's Gallon in *London*, which the Drawer interprets but half a Pint. As they never speak as they think, their false Tongues may be compar'd to the Cards at *Primiviste*, in which Game 6 is 18, and 7 is 21. The poorer sort have a piece of Linnen peeping out at their Collars for show of a Shirt; but with long wearing it is so black and ragged, that it is going to the Paper-Mill as fast as it can. When the Beasts enter'd into the Ark by *Pairs*, I wonder how *Noah* coupl'd the *Scots*, for they are strange Creatures both by Sea and Land; and an Ass is scarce to be had in this Nation either for Love or Money, because they put 'em all into Commissions of the Peace. They retain one barbarous Custom still, and that is, if any two be displeas'd they expect no Law, but bang it out, one and his kindred against the other and his; being so implacable in their hatred, that on each side they use a Scale of Destruction, by striving to ruin the Father, beggar the Son, and strangle the Hopes of all Posterity: And this Fighting they call their *Feider*, a Word so barbarous, that was it to be express'd in *Latin*, it must be by Circumlocution.

Their ill Manners make them look more salvage than the Monsters put by *Astrologers* to the Humane Limbs in *Anatomy*; wherefore it is strange that *Physicians* do not apply a *Scotchman* to the Soles of the Feet in a desperate Fever, for he would draw far beyond Pidgeons; and it is thought some of our *English* Quacks, Empericks or Mountebanks will slice one to try the Experiment. The *Scots* were ever as great Friends to the King of *France*, as *Don Quixot* was to *Sancho Pancho*, who fought at all Adventures to purchase the other the Government of an Island which was none of his; and they think themselves as brave Fellows as the *Spanish* Knight Errant, when he fought a Windmill, to the great Danger of breaking the Necks of him and his Horse *Rosinante*, when it flung 'em both into a Pond. Their Godliness is of the same Parentage with good Laws, both extracted out of bad Manners; and their Teachers live upon the Sins of their Congregations, which verifies the Axiom, *Iisdem nutritur ex quibus componitur.* They dread to be civiliz'd; and they have a great Antipathy against Church Windows which are painted, when a Looking Glass would shew them more Superstition: In fine, a *Scotchman* is such a Hater of Images, that he hath defac'd God's in his own Countenance.

THE COMICAL PILGRIM'S PILGRIMAGE
INTO IRELAND.

aving seen too much Villany in *Scotland* to pay the least Adoration to the Country, I return'd to *London* again, and after a short Stay there went for *Highlake* in *Cheshire*, where going on Board the *Seaforth* Gally, Sail was presently hoisted, and in a few Hours bidding Adieu to the Sight of Old *England* and *Wales*, we came to Anchor in the Bay of *Dublin* very early on a *Whitsun-Monday* in the Morning. Here I went ashore at *Dunlary*, and being got safe in that Part of *Terræ firmæ*, which, I think, is situated *in podice Mundi*, I went Five Miles farther to *D U B L I N*, the Metropolis of *Ireland*, standing on the *Liffie* River, as well as the Sea. This Country is seperated from *England* by a very dangerous Sea, in which meeting with a most dreadful Hurricane, as soon as the tempestuous Weather was over, my *Muse* incited me to delineate the Seamens Devotion in bad Weather, in the following Meditation.

When Nature shews the Seaman various Forms
Of Death, in Tempests, Hurricanes, and Storms,
The Ship in Danger, Master, or the Mate,
Cries, Reef the Sails before it is too late;
We cannot bear 'em in this Stress of Weather,
Up nimbly, Boys, G—— d—— you, all together.
A Sailor from the Fore-Mast-Top bauls out,
By G—— there'll be no Calm to Day, I doubt;
Then answers one, who's on the Main-Yard Arm,
Z——ds, Lads, as yet we have receiv'd no Harm.
But next another cries, G—— d—— my Soul,
How cursedly the rotten Bitch do's rowl!
Whilst here do's split a Mast, there rent a Sail,
Another swears, by Heav'n the Ship do's fail:
Some cry, G—— rot us, we shall all be drown'd,
The very Storm do's rage the Compass round;
For steer which Way we will, the Wind do's blow
Contrary to the Course we strive to go.
But hark! below Deck next a Man do's speak,
And briskly swears, the Vessel springs a-leak;
Then how the Seamen helter-skelter jump,

> *To save the Ship and Cargo by the Pump;*
> *Which useless grown, the Master says, I think*
> *The Vessel founders, we begin to sink.*
> *D——n ye, hoist out the Long-Boat, Wind defies*
> *Our Art, the Gunhil under Water lies;*
> *Come, leave the Whip-Staff; Lads, make hast, G——'s B——*
> *Your Luffs nor Ports can do us now no Good.*
> *Mean while the Chaplain, who shou'd for 'em pray,*
> *Instead of praying, swears as fast as they:*
> *And just on drowning, in one hideous Yell,*
> *They curse their Fate, and swim with speed to Hell.*

But being got upon firm Land again, as I said before, I was very glad of visiting the *Irish* Natives, tho' they are not yet wholly brought to a civil Course of Life, thro' the Fathers inflicting an heavy Curse on all their Posterity, if ever they should sow Corn, build Houses, or learn the *English* Tongue: And the Reason of this inveterate Antipathy is, because heretofore there being but one Freeholder in a whole County, which was the Lord himself, the rest held in Villanage; and being subject to the Lord's immeasurable Taxations, they had no Encouragement to build, sow, or plant. *Ireland* is divided into 4 Provinces; namely, *Munster*; *Leinster*, where *Stonehenge* once stood, but by *Magick* Art *Merlin* remov'd those ponderous Stones out of this Territory into *Wiltshire*; *Connaught*, where are some Vines, but rather serving for Shade than Profit, for in these Parts the Sun entring into *Virgo*, causeth cold Gales to blow, and in Autumn the Afternoon's Heat is so faint and short, that it cannot ripen the Clusters; and *Ulster*, whose antient Custom in making their King was by taking a white Cow, which his *Irish* Majesty must kill, and seeth the same in Water whole, then must he bath himself therein stark naked; and sitting in the Caldron wherein it is sod, accompanied with the People round about him, he and they eat the Flesh, and drink the Broth (much Good may't do 'em) without Cup, Dish or Spoon. No sooner was I arriv'd at *Dublin*, but being in Company with some Collegians of *Trinity-College* there, which is all the Colleges their University contains, they to shew their extraordinary Parts to me a Stranger in a poetick Way, made Verses *ex tempore*, and I to Oblige them writ off of Hand the following Lines.

> *When pious* Israel, *by* Jehovah *blest,*
> *Had been four hundred Years and more opprest,*
> *By haughty* Pharaoh's *arbitrary Sway,*
> *Which Doom'd the* Hebrew *Vassals to Obey,*
> *It pleas'd the Pow'r of an Almighty Hand*
> *To Scourge a stubborn King, and sinful Land,*
> *With ten afflictions, grievous to a Realm,*
> *Where Pride and Superstition sat at Helm.*
> *Yet Wrath Divine was not so much Display'd,*
> *To make a wise Creator be Obey'd,*
> *But that indulging Heaven kept in store,*
> *For* Ireland, *a dozen Plagues and more.*
> *Nits make their Youths, before they're Old, look Grey,*

And rampant Lice upon their Bodies Prey;
Their Summer Visiters are Swarms of Fleas,
Which Sting the Females that they can't have Ease.
Poverty Nips 'em, Ign'rance is their Guide,
And Sloth in Triumph thro' their Cabbins ride.
Misery for lazy Lives they Celebrate;
And Loyalty (which proves their Ruin) hate.
Their chiefest Talent much in Nonsense lies;
And honest Principles they all Dispise.
Devotion is a Stranger to their Thoughts,
And small Temptations make their Women Morts.
But that which adds to their intailed Curse,
Is store of Children, but an empty Purse.
Thus, if these are not Plagues enough, may Pox,
And all the Ails which cram'd Pandora's *Box,*
Always severely Torture them; and be
The Portion of their wild Posterity.

This Satyr being Truth and Matter of Fact, how well it pleas'd the *Irish* Collegians may be easily guess'd, however taking leave of my learned Company, I went out to look about me in the City, where I star'd and gap'd around, like our Country Hicks upon the Signs in *London*, the Monument, or Tombs in *Westminster-Abby*. *Ringsend* Coaches, so call'd from a Place of that Name about a Mile or two out of the *Dublinian* Suburbs, I saw were more numerous than Hackney or Gentlemen's Coaches; and which being a sort of Carts made with a Seat before, wherein People may be jolted 3 or 4 Miles for 2 Pence, your topping City Cuckolds and their Wives very often ride out of Town in 'em, to make a Demolition of Cakes and Ale. Being mounted next upon *Lousie-Hill*, and asking whence the Place deriv'd its Name, some knowing People inform'd me, that an old Woman once dwelling there, to whom honest St. *Patrick*, a Swineherd, and tutelary Patron of that Kingdom promis'd to clear that Nation of Lice, she fell a weeping, and humbly besought the good old Man not to destroy them, because the Inhabitants had no other Diversion on *Sundays*, than to sit at home and louse themselves; whereupon her Request being granted, the *Irish* enjoy the Company of their native Cattle to this Day, in Memory of which peculiar Favour this Street ever since bears the Name of *Lousie-Hill*. At last I rambled into *Smock-Alley*, where the *Irish* Theatre is situated; Curiosity led me soon into it, when *Dryden's* Opera, call'd King *Arthur*, was to be acted, which is a Play I lik'd well enough, excepting these two Lines in Act I. Scene I.

On yon proud Towers, before the Day be done,
My glittering Banners shall be wav'd against the setting Sun.

For tho' the *Greek* and *Latin* Poets, in their Compositions, made their *Hexameter* or *Heroick* Verse, compos'd of *Dactyls* and *Spondees*, yet always observing to have each Line to end with an *Adonick* likewise, it runs smoother than what our Language will with 15 or more Syllables, for we cannot exceed 10 Feet, or 12 at the most, without offending a delicate Ear.

Farther, let me observe, that the *Irish* Stage is now as much cumber'd as the

English Stage, with Inventions not used in former Ages; I mean with *Opera's* and *Farce*; the first stupifying the Audience in such a quivering Manner in their Songs, that the Words and Sense too are both lost in the Tune: And the other is a Representation of Things not natural, and is but one, or 3 Acts at most; contrary to the Rule of dramatick Poetry, which, *Horace* says in his Book *de Arte Poetica*, must have no more or less than 5 Acts. As for *Comedy*, it is as much, nay more corrupted in *Ireland*, than in *England*, *France* or *Italy*, in too much admitting the *Mimick* in the *Drama*: And let me tell you (tho' a Pilgrim) that since I am enter'd upon this Discourse, I must take Notice, that tho' *Comedy* is an Imitation of inferior People in Ridicule, yet ought not the Ridicule to be extravagant, but gracefully and slightly touch'd, as by *Terence* in his Pieces. Again, altho *Comedy* represents low Persons, yet are they not the meanest, since it brings eminent Citizens and Magistrates on the Stage; nay, *Plautus* in his *Amphytrio* introduces Gods and Kings, but nevertheless it is a true *Comedy*, because he hath turn'd the Subject of *Tragedy* into Ridicule; and it looks beautiful enough, if the Actors have a Regard to their Pronunciation and Gesture, according to *Quintilian*'s Rule, in the 11th Chapter of his First Book which is this: *Debet etiam docere comœdus quomodo narrandum*, &c. That is, a *Comedian* ought to teach how we should speak, with what Authority we should persuade, with what Emotion Anger should be rais'd, and with what Change of Voice we may excite Pity: I can't blame those who spend some Time with the Masters of the palestrick Art; that is, those who form the Gestures and Motions, teach how to hold the Arms, and the Hands, that we seem not to be rustick, or ignorant, to have no unseemly Carriage, no unbecoming Posture of the Feet, and that the Head and Eyes don't differ from the other Motions of the Body. But these Rules are no where strictly observ'd by Players: Moreover, as the Design of *Comedy* is to rectify the Manners of Men and Women, nothing ought to be represented which may vitiate the Audience, for the People being generally the same, they obstinately retain the most licentious and obscene Things; especially when they are impiously joyn'd to Religion. Indeed *Ben Johnson* is often guilty of this Fault in his *Volpone*, especially where he brings in Sir *Politick Would be* talking thus prophanely to *Peregrine*.

> *And then, for your Religion, profess none;*
> *But wonder at the Diversity of all.*　　　　　　　　Act 4. Sc. 1.

Also *Ben Johnson* in his *Alchymist* so much dishonours his Maker, as to suffer the most tremendous Name of God to be made so vile and cheap, as to be us'd often as an expletive Particle to prevent a Chasme, or make up a Gap in a Sentence, that it may run more smoothly; as appears by some of his Persons thus speaking.

> *God's Will then, Queen of Fairies*
> *On with your Tire; and, Doctor, with your Robes.*
> *Let's dispatch him for God's sake.*　　　　　　　　Act 3. Sc. 3.

> *Fore God,*
> *She is a delicate Dab chick! I must have her.*　　　　　　　　Act 4. Scen. 2.

As for *Tragedies*, those are the most perfect ones in which there are *Peripeties*, that is, Revolutions, Changes of Fortune, and Remembrances, as in the *Oedipus* of *Sophocles*, the first *Tragedy* of all Antiquity, where in the 3d Scene of the 4th

Act, the *Peripetie*, or Change of one Fortune into another, is contrary to what was expected, in the Man that comes from *Corinth* to acquaint *Oedipus* of the Death of King *Polybius*. I shall not take Notice of the Duration of the Representation of a *Play*, which ought not to exceed the Space of a natural Day; but observe, that the Sect of the *Peripateticks* believing neither *Providence* nor *fatal Necessity*, but imputes all Accidents to Chance, the antient tragick *Poets* chose rather to follow the Opinion of the *Stoicks*, who acknowledge a *Providence* and fatal Necessity; as very well perceiving, that that was the only Means to preserve the *Theatre*, those wonderful Surprizes, which are produc'd by Accidents that seem fortuitous, and yet nevertheless have Causes assign'd to them, which are certain. Again, it is to be noted, that the *Prologue* should be plac'd before the Play; but *Plautus* hath took the Liberty of the *Greeks*, in placing the Prologue in the Play, as particularly in the first Act of his *Miles gloriosus*, and after the first Act in *Cistellaria*; however, as I hint above, this Custom ought not to be follow'd by any prudent and regular Poet; and therefore *Terence* hath took Care not to be guilty of so great a Fault. The *Catastrophe* of a Play must be happy or fatal; but *Euripides* has made his Pieces to have a miserable one, wherefore he appears to be the most tragical of all the *Poets*. Now the Use of Machines, which makes the Gods and Goddesses appear upon the Stage, is founded on the generally received Opinion of the *Ethnichs*, who suppose the Gods can see all things, and take Care of Men; for if there were none but *Epicureans* in the World, the Machines would be ridiculous, or not suffer'd, because they would directly thwart their Opinion, in affirming the Gods lead a quiet Life, free from all Sorts of Care, and if *Nature* sometimes doth those Things which seem miraculous, the Gods take no Notice of it, and don't interrupt their Pleasure. By the Way also I must note, that the Imitation of Lightning and Thunder may be put into the Number of the Machines, and also that furious Storm, which makes the unravelling of the second *Oedipus* in *Sophocles*; for altho' *Jupiter* doth not appear, yet 'tis he who sends that Tempest, during which *Oedipus* is buried: And from hence I infer, that Machines may be employ'd, not only out of, but also in the Action of Tragedy, provided there be an absolute Necessity for them.

But many of our modern *Dramatists* have not exactly observ'd the aforesaid Discourse, or kept themselves strictly to the Unity of Action, Time, and Place. For *Shakespear* in his Tragedy of *Othello*, the *Moor* of *Venice*, makes the Duration of what he represents to be above 3 Weeks or a Month; I think the Representation of his Play begins in *Italy*, whence his black General went to *Cyprus*, an Island on the Coast of *Syria*, and to which he could not well arrive under a Fortnight, according as the Storm he met with held longer or shorter. The Absurdities and Blunders of this illiterate *Poetaster* being so many, that whatever he writ was not worth acting in *Bartholomew* Fair, I shall only take Notice of the little Knowledge he had in *Astronomy*, when in Act 1. Scen. 2. he says,

> *For do but stand upon the foaming Shore,*
> *The chiding Billows seem to pelt the Clouds,*
> *The Wind shake Surge, with high and monst'rous Main,*
> *Seems to cast Water on the burning Bear,*
> *And quench the Guards of the ever-fired Pole.*

In these Lines I reckon he hath given a false *Epithet* to the *Bear*, which ought to have been *lesser* instead of *burning*, by talking of the *Guards* presently after, which are the two foremost Stars in *Ursa minor*, whereof that which is in the Shoulder of this Constellation, hath Longitude 128 Degrees, 23 Minutes, and North Latitude 72 Degrees, 40 Minutes, insomuch that being nearest of all the Northern Constellations to the North Pole, I wonder how there can be any extraordinary Heat within the frigid Zone. Also in the same Play he supposes the Soul to be the Production of some mortal Substance, according to these Words of *Emilia*, Act 5. Scen. 1.

> *If he say so, may his pernicious Soul*
> *Rot half a Grain a-day.*

But *Shakespear* being no Scholar, I suppose he had so little Skill in *Rhetorick*, that by a *Synecdoche* he did not put a *Whole* for a Part, as *Virgil* do's *Anima* for *Homo*, in describing the Funeral of *Polydorus*, in *Æneid. lib. 3*. The Faults of this same *Poetaster* are not a few also in his *Tragedy*, call'd *Hamlet*, Prince of *Denmark*; in which he is mighty drolling, particularly where he tells an old Woman's Story of the Cocks crowing always at *Christmas*, in Act 1. Scen. 1.

> *It faded at the Crowing of the Cock.*
> *Some say, that ever 'gainst that Season comes,*
> *Wherein our Saviour's Birth is Celebrated,*
> *This Bird of dawning singeth all Night long,*
> *And then, they say, no Spirit dares stir abroad,*
> *The Nights are wholsome; then no Plannets strike,*
> *No Fairy takes, no Witch hath Power to Charm,*
> *So hallow'd and so gracious is that Time.*

Truly Mr. *Lee* was in my Opinion, the most exact of all our modern *Dramatists* in his Plays; but yet he is not without his Irregularities and Foibles, especially in religious Matters, of which we shall only take notice of this in his *Tragedy* call *Theodosius*, or the Force of Love, where, in Act 3. Scen. 1. he represents the Emperor *Theodosius* a hopeful Convert, when at the sight of *Athenais* he makes one of the Articles of the Christian Faith a *Simile* for his Cod-piece Passion in these Words,

> *What hinders now but in spite of Rules*
> *I burst thro' all the Bands of Death that hold me,*
> *And fly with such a haste to that Appearance,*
> *As bury'd Saints shall make at the last Summons.*

In Mr. *Lee*'s Tragedy call'd the Rival Queens, or the Death of *Alexander* the Great, in Act 1. Scen. I. he makes *Polyperchon* give a Description of Hell after the *Christian* Manner; for tho' it was the *Theology* of the *Grecians* to believe a future State, yet it does not occur to my Memory that I ever read they allotted any Punishment to the Wicked by Fire, as he intimates in these Lines.

> *Tho' the Earth yawn so wide,*
> *That all the Labours of the Deep were seen,*
> *And* Alexander *stood on the other Side,*
> *I'd leap the burning Ditch to give him Death,*
> *Or sink my self for ever.*

And in Act 4. Scen. I. he introduces *Cassander* speaking so prophanely, that it must rather vitiate the Audience than make them virtuous.

> *'Tis nobler far to be a King of Hell,*
> *To Head infernal Legions, Chiefs below,*
> *To let 'em loose for Earth, to call 'em in,*
> *And take Account of what dark Deeds are done,*
> *Than be a Subject God in Heav'n unblest,*
> *And without Mischief have eternal Rest.*

As for Mr. *Shadwell*, he hath mixt his Tragedy call'd the *Libertine* with so much Comedy, that the Play is rather tragi-comical than tragical; tho' there is Blood enough spilt in it which might, with good Husbandry, serve very well for two or three Tragedies: But to make Don *John* the Libertine talk of a Soul in Act I. when an Atheist believes no such Thing existing in a Man, it is very absurd, as you may see in the following Lines, which plainly describe the Person's Character.

> *Let's on, and live the nobler Life of Sense;*
> *To all the Powers of Love and mighty Lust,*
> *In spite of formal Fops I will be just.*
> *What Ways soe'er conduce to my Delight,*
> *My Sense instructs me, I must think 'em right.*
> *On, on my Soul, and make no Stop in Pleasure,*
> *They're dull insipid Fools, who live by Measure.*

Was I to criticise on all the Errors occurring in the *Greek*, *Latin* and *English* Dramatists, I should swell my Criticisms to a Bulk exceeding these swelling Expressions of *Seneca*, in the first Act of his *Hercules Oetæus*, whom he makes to speak in these bragging, bouncing, and ranting Strains.

> *Vel si times ne terra concipiat feras,*
> *Properet malum quodcunque dum terra Herculem*
> *Habet, videtque.*
> *Da, da tuendos Jupiter saltem deos:*
> *Illa licebit fulmina parte auferas,*
> *Ego quam tuebor: sive glacialem polum,*
> *Seu me tueri fervidam partem jubes,*
> *Hac esse superos parte securos puta.*

By these Lines we plainly see how miserable *Jupiter* must be, who cannot be safe from wild Beasts without an *Hercules*; and then again how little and weak the *Poet* makes the Gods, in representing them to stand in Need of Human Help: But the tragick *Poets* do very often err in this Manner, by extolling Things above Nature. Moreover, altho' some Morality may be learnt by the Judicious either from tragick or comick Writers, yet there are none of the dramatick Poets but what have too much Immorality and Prophaness in their Writings; and hence it follows that either *Tragedy* or *Comedy*, as being a Representation of Things, must be of a more pernicious Consequence than an *Epick* Poem, which is only a Recitation. A dramatick *Poet* must make the Person which he brings on the Stage to speak exactly to the Character which he or she represents: Thus whether the Person that represents another, is to act the Part of a Tyrant, Adulterer, Villain, Drunkard, or any other wicked profligate Wretch, as the Humour of such Persons must be represented always the same, without any Variety, the Representation of such notorious Crimes may be of an ill Consequence to green Heads; and especially in being Spectators of such Plays, which treat of those Subjects whose Stories are taken from, or belonging to Hell. Farthermore there is as much Buffoonry and Drollery acted on the *Irish* Stage as on the *English* Stage, as having *Harlequins* shewing *Merry-Andrew*'s Tricks; *Scaramouches* jumping into Barrels; Dame *Ragonda* skipping about with 9 Brats at her Heels; or a brainless Fellow, who has more Grimace than Sense, riding upon an Ass, which (I'm sure) is false Heraldry to put Metal upon Metal.

But being as soon tir'd of *Dublin*, as a *Drury-Lane* Strumpet is of Beetle and Punny in *Bridewell*, I left that lewd Town to visit the Country; accordingly I went to *Manooth*, a Town in the County of *Kildare*, where I saw nothing memorable, but an old Castle much ruinated by the famous Usurper *Oliver Cromwell*, of inglorious Memory. Hence I went to *Kilcock*, a Mile beyond which is a Stone-Mill, said to be built by the Devil; and truly by its strange Contrivance, I'm apt to believe it may be the Workmanship of some infernal Artist. Four Miles forward is *Clenard*, on the Skirts of which Town is a Bridge over the River *Boyn*; memorable for the entire Defeat King *William* gave his Royal Competitor for the Diadem of three Kingdoms. Hence I went to *Mullingar*; and from thence to *Balimore*, otherwise call'd *Balimore-Lough-Sunderland*, or *Sivedelie*, in the County of *West-Meath*; but how improper the Derivation is in one Respect, as well as incredulous in another, I leave to your judicious Sense to determine; for *Bali* signifies a Town in the *Bogtrotters Jargon*, and *More*, great; which *Epithet* is not at all suitable to this Place, when there are scarce 40 Houses in it. But then again to name it *Sunderland*, or *Sivedelie*, which signifies a Beetle to beat wet Linnen, the Accident I am going to recite, methinks could not impose upon the Faith of any but a *Papist*, who makes Traditions an essential Part of his *Credo*; for as I was inform'd by some dwelling here, there goes a Story of a Maid, living in former Ages, when a Grove grew where this Lough now is, on the North Side of the Town, with a small Brook running thro' it; and one Day washing in this solitary Place, and accidentally dropping her Beetle into the Water, the Trees in the Grove instantly vanished, and the Ground became a large Lough: Thus by giving too much Credulity to a Lie, this Town begot a Name as long as a *Spanish* Nobleman's. In the Church-Yard here I took Notice of a Grave-stone, on which was this insignificant Inscription: *Pray for the Soul of Major* John Duneel, *who departed the 6th of* November, 1694; *as also for his Wife* Elizabeth Jones; *and his Sons* Henry, William *and* Richard, *who caused this Tomb to be made*, Anno Domini 1696. And under it carv'd *J. H. S.* the Initial Letters of, *Iesus Hominum Salvator*. Not far from this is another Grave stone over a Miller, with all the chief Tools of his thieving Occupation carv'd thereon: And this Mode I saw was pretty customary among Tradesmen in many Church-Yards in this Kingdom.

Next I went to *Athlone*, a Town not only situated in the two Provinces of *Leinster* and *Connought*, but also in the two Counties of *West-Meath* and *Roscommon*. The *Shannon*, the largest River in *Ireland*, running from North to South, divides it into two Parts; over which is a Stone Bridge, containing seven Arches, built by old Queen *Bess*; and on it is cut out a Man and Dog with this Inscription. Robarts Damport *Was Overseer of this Workys*. Indeed, the Matter is not so material as to be worthy of communicating it to the Publick, but only to let my Readers see their antient way of Spelling, which is not much different from the modern *Orthography* now in use among 'em; and to delineate the Arrogancy of this petty Officer, who, because *Alexander* the Great respected his Horse *Bucephalus*, attempted to immortalize his *Irish* Cur too. Hence I went to *Balidagon*, a little Village six Miles from *Athlone*; but whence this Place takes its Name I cant imagine, unless a Remnant of the cursed *Philistines* made their Escape from the Slaughtering *Israelites*, by Swimming over the Sea; and settling in this bye Country, they dedicated these Receptacles of Poverty to their Monstrous God, *Dagon*. Proceeding onwards on my Pilgrimage, I went to *Balinasloe*; the People of which small Town are so Zealous, that rather than want a House of Devotion, they assemble in a little Cabbin, where a Bank is raised for the Bog-trotting Congregation to sit on; and such an awkward Pulpit, Desk, and Communion-Table is bestow'd on the poor *Levite*, that it would puzzle Ingenuity to fathom the Depth of humane Fancy for their true Description: However, taking some Pity and Compassion on these godly Wretches, before I left 'em I compil'd for them the following Stanza's, call'd

The Irish LITANY.

From a Country full of Rebellion and Treason;
From a People not Honest, and void of all Reason;
From running of Goods, which is ne'er out of Season;
Libera nos, Domine.

From dry'd up Potatoes, without any Butter;
From unwholesome Water, which gives the wild Squtter;
From Priests, who in Latin *to Blockheads do mutter;*
Libera nos, Domine.

From Women whose Features wou'd frighten the Devil;
From Children whose Skin's like an Orange of Sevil;
And are bred from the Womb to all manner of Evil;
Libera nos, Domine.

From thick Bonny-clabber, a Med'cine for Witches;
From Usquebaugh, *loved by all drunken Bitches;*
From Vermin, which makes 'em scratch where it Itches;
Libera nos, Domine.

From getting of Children, but nothing to keep 'em;
From Corn-Fields, where idle Lubbers won't reap 'em;
From Fleas, where People by Bushels may weep 'em;
Libera nos, Domine.

From wretchedly living in our poor Condition;
From Beggars, whose Pride for great Places petition;
Or else from the Dunghil wou'd bear a Commission.
Libera nos, Domine.

From Mayors, full as foolish as guzling Churchwardens,
From Dublin, *full of Whores as the* Spring-Gardens;
From a Papist, *whose Heart against* Protestants *hardens;*
Libera nos, Domine.

From running o'er Bogs, in all sorts of Weather,
From wearing flat Brogues, made of nasty hard Leather,
From wearing slight Trowsers, which scarce hang together;
Libera nos, Domine.

From going bare-foot, both Summer and Winter;
From wearing a Smock till it's whiter than Tinder;
From Poets, *whose Parts will never reach* Pindar;
Libera nos, Domine.

From Knights of the Post against Innocents swearing,
From Doxies, whose Mouths for raw Flesh are staring;
And from their Presumption of Mens Breeches wearing;
Libera nos, Domine.

From Lice, Itch, and Scabs, the Plague of our Nation;
From Pimps, who claim rich Men for a Relation;
And from our blind Way of gaining Salvation;
Libera nos, Domine.

From Cook-Maids as nasty as any Gold finder;
From Pastors as blind as a Beetle and blinder;
From Strumpets, whom Money make never the kinder,
Libera nos, Domine.

From trading with France, *to get ourselves Riches;*
From often cooling our Courage in Ditches;
T'asswage the rebellious Flesh in the Breeches;
Libera nos, Domine.

From Blind leading blind Folks, and Criples the Criple;
From going to Church without any Steeple;
From Ropes without Bells, to ring in the People;
Libera nos, Domine.

From Rapparees medling with Travellers Purses;
From Servants as base as damn'd Parish Nurses;
From Teaguelanders full of Damnation and Curses.
Libera nos, Domine.

Bidding adieu to *Balinosloe,* I went to *Aghrim,* where the Number of Houses exceed not a Pair-Royal of Aces; however, the Place will be ever memorable in History, for the decisive Battle fought here, which reduced a whole Kingdom to the Obedience of the *Protestant* King *William.* And all over the Plain here lie scatter'd Heaps of Mens Sculls to this Day; insomuch that it does not only represent *Golgotha,* but had also the Father of that *Grecian* Hero dwelt here, who wept for more Worlds to add to his Conquests, he might have sav'd his Page the Labour of shewing him at Meals the ghastful Emblem of Mortality. Hence I proceeded to *Loghrea*, where is kept the chiefest Market in all the Province of *Connaught*; and from thence going to *Killilel*, I saw a small wooden Cross set tottering upon a Heap of Stones in the Road; about which some Priest, and his bigotted Tribe, had been mumbling a *Pater Noster*, and *Ave Maria* to the Blessed Lady. At *Balihavely* I took Notice of an old Castle metamorphosed into a Cow-House; and next I went to *Athenrea*, an ancient, but much ruinated Town, built by old King *John* of merry Memory. Then I came to *Galway*, a large Seaport Town, situated on the River *Caarle*; when I first enter'd this Place, I really took it to be a general Goal for the whole Kingdom; for the Houses (which are some one, some two, and some three Stories high) are all strongly built of Stone, and most of the Windows thick barricadoed with thick Iron Bars, insomuch that there are not the like Buildings to be seen through the Country for Strength. In the Midst of this Town stands a Church, dedicated to honest St. *Nicholas*, whose Steeple hath a pretty good Set of Bells, and its Chimes are somewhat Musical, but not well approv'd by the *Fanaticks*, because they are set to the Tune of a *Psalm*. Moreover, in this Church are two Pulpits, one for the Doctor to preach in, and one for the Archbishop of *Tuam*, in case his Preferment makes him not above it.

The Women of this Country are generally so homely, that had the Mother of all Living been as ugly, when she took her ill-condition'd Being from one of Father *Adam*'s Ribs, her frightful Phisiognomy had forc'd the Godhead to act the sixth Day over again. Seeing the female Sex so ordinary, to comfort them under this Misfortune, I composed the following Lines, call'd the Picture of an *Irish* Woman.

> *Of all the Creatures I have ever found,*
> *An* Irish *Woman is a strange Compound!*
> *Unseemly Gestures wanton Sports betray,*
> *Yet talk of Love, she knows not what to say.*
> *Her chiefest Breeding lies in milking Cows,*
> *Her Face is only fit to fright the Crows;*
> *Her Breasts are large, her Belly somewhat hard,*
> *And Modesty's a Thing she'll ne'er regard:*
> *But yet to give the* Teagueland *Beast her Due,*
> *Her Skin is really a* Mulatto's *Hue;*
> *Ugly's her Hand, yet Legs so little be,*
> *That litler Mill-Posts you shall seldom see.*
> *Her roving Eyes lascivious Looks betray,*
> *And as the Night obscures a glorious Day,*
> *So Ragged Mantles, or a Cloak do's hide*
> *Those Imperfections which we should deride.*
> *Splavin's her Foot, irregular her Nose,*
> *Which always is uncleanly as her Cloaths;*
> *Her Buttocks swell, like lustful Bull his Cod,*
> *And Knees are never bended to her God:*
> *For, when at Leisure, her Devotion's most*
> *Bestow'd on Priest, and consecrated Host.*

Her Speech discovers a perfidious Heart,
The which on very easie Terms she'll part;
And as for that strange Cup which Water keeps
With downward Mouth, awake, or when she sleeps,
Let her be honest Woman, Maid, or Whore,
Like Death and Hell 'tis gaping still for more.

But yet for all this Dearth of handsome Women, this Country in another Respect is far happier than *England*, as being less infected with *Lawyers*, that common Bane of all Mankind. The wild *Irish*, in all Courts of Judicature, are sworn upon a Scull; herein being more scrupulous of forswearing themselves, than by taking a false Oath on the *New-Testament*; as supposing the Ghost to whom that Scull once pertain'd would haunt them, in case they prov'd perjur'd. Assizes are held twice a Year for criminal Matters, and Cases of *Nisi prius*; and tho' *Astræa* left no Print of her Footsteps in this Nation when she fled to Heaven, yet so partial is blindfold Justice here betwixt Man and Beast, that the Stone Pounds for offending Cattle seem stronger built than Goals for Malefactors. Murderers are hang'd and quarter'd; and *Rapparees* share the same Fate: Which last in former Times was the *Militia* of the Country, but the mean Souls of the *Irish* detesting now what is honourable and Praiseworthy, to follow Theft, this martial Denomination suffers the same hard Fate with those honest Names of *Tyrant* and *Sophister*, which from Titles of Honour are degenerated into Terms of the greatest Disgrace and Infamy; for a *Rapparee* now signifies no more than a Robber on the Highway. As for the great Commerce the People drives, that was plainly perceiv'd by meeting neither Waggon nor Pack-Horse 100 Miles an End. The wild Native *Irish* observe more Days of Fasting and Abstinence than the Rubrick of their Church enjoyns them; because extream Poverty excludes them from the Use of Flesh and Fowl from one Year's End to another. Their Lodging is in small Cabbins, without Chimneys, put up in the Highways; and in these the Man, his Wife and Children, Cocks, Hens, Chickens, Hogs, Pigs, Cows, Calves and Geese lie all together. If *Teague* is so topping as to rent a small Potatoe-Garden for 5 Shillings *per Annum*, he thinks himself as well to pass as that *Italian* Duke, who's married Yearly to the *Adriatic* Sea; however, his Tenement shall be no better furnish'd than the rest of his Neighbours; which is commonly set off with a Truss of Straw to lie on, a Grid-Iron, and Pot to boil *Potatoes*. These wild People wear neither Shoes nor Stockings, which makes me strongly to suspect that they are born without any, as Monsieur *Ragou*'s Bastard was without a Shirt; and as often as I behold their tatter'd Apparel, which scarce covers what Modesty ought to conceal, I imagine them to proceed from the Loyns of *Ham*, who discovering his Father's Nakedness, the Curse of him and his Posterity lay in never being well cloath'd again.

Here are no Stage-Coaches; and instead of Carts they use only little Cars, with small Wheels without Spokes, so that they cannot carry above 3 or 400 Weight of Tallow, which is one of the chiefest Commodities of this Country. Sliding Carts are also very common, imitating much our Halliers in *Bristol*. Instead of Soap they use *Cackmacrel*, that is, the Excrements of Dogs whether thick or thin, which poor Women gather up in the Streets with as great Pains as they do Rags in *London*. In

England Women ride upon the left Side of a Horse, but here they ride upon the wrong Side; and very often astride. Most Things edible or potable are very cheap; but why is that? Because Money is scarce, which makes an *English* Shillings go for 13 Pence, and a Guinea 1 Pound 3 Shillings, which is considerable above their intrinsick Value. The Inhabitants of this Kingdom greatly admire a Dish of Potatoes, to which they have such an Appetite, that I believe they long for 'em after they are dead; for in most Potatoe-Gardens many Souls, grinning strangely at this delicious Food, which is both Bread and Meat to an *Irishman*; but whether they get thither by Accident, or some sympathetical Vertue, whose strange Effect proceeding from as strange a Cause, the Relicks of their mortal Carcasses will insensibly creep (like the Sun's Shadow on a Dial) to what they most affected in this Lite, is a Subject on which I shall not insist. For above 40 Miles together I could not see a Stack of Hay; and Beasts are very small here, excepting the Woman, who being great Breeders, stand hard and fast by that primary Command, *Increase and multiply*; but I suppose their Obedience to this Precept is more by natural Instinct, than acquir'd by any Knowledge of the Scriptures, to which they are as meer Strangers as the remotest Heathens. So boggy is most part of the Country, that if it is not *Lucifer's* Backside, one may very reasonably impute it to be the grand Magazine of Nature's Impurity. Popery is very predominant; for altho' severe Acts are made against Jesuits, Monks, and Fryers, yet secular Priests, who own no Ecclesiastical Jurisdiction of the See of *Rome*, are tolerated to say Mass. Besides, several private Nunneries, the *Papists* have public Chapels here; one about a Furlong or two without the West-Gate of *Galway*, dedicated to the Virgin *Mary*; and another a little without Abby-Gate, dedicated to St. *Francis*. Superstition has a great Ascendant over their Faith; for about half a Mile without *William's* Gate are two Wells, dedicated to the blessed Lady and St. *Tavison*, round which every *Sunday* Morning they walk barefoot an Hour together, mumbling over their Beads, and then crossing themselves with the Water, which they hold to be good against several Infirmities, they return home as little sanctified as they went. The Pulpit-Prayers us'd by the *Protestant* Clergy in *Ireland*, are scarce as long as the Lord's Prayer and Doxology; for they are all as idle as our *English* Parsons, who don't preach, but read Sermons, excepting here and there one that scorns to teach his Congregation out of a Book.

From *Galway* I went to *Carmorris*, on the left Hand whereof are several Houses paying Tribute to the Ruins of Fire and Sword. Next I went to *Balihove*, in the County of *Mayo*; and truly of all the *Irish* Counties commend me to this for good Fellowship; for here they will kill one another to raise a Rundlet of *Aqua-vitæ*. As passing through this Country, I overtook a little Car loaded with this Liquor, which they prefer above their beloved *Usquebaugh*, drawing before a Corpse; and as soon as the senseless Clod was interr'd in an obscure Place among Bogs and Hills, they fell heartily to their strong Sippings, which they drew out into square wooden Cups, and thence took it out agen with Egg-shels, which serv'd instead of Tasters. For my part being a Stranger, they invited me to participate of their Liquor; accordingly I tarried with them, to see their Manners; 'till the Spirits flew so much into their Heads, that one Brother in a Quarrel kill'd another. Hereupon some were for carrying him to Justice, and others again for hiding the bloody Fact; thus whilst a long Controversie held concerning what to do in this tragical Matter, an old Man among 'em starts up, and addresses himself as follows.

"Loving Friends and Acquaintance, in taking our last Farewel of a Neighbour here departed, the Funeral Meeting has unhappily occasion'd the Loss of another. Now if we should deliver up this Criminal to the Government, the Severity of their Justice will deprive us of a third Friend; which Punishment will not retrieve the Life of his unfortunate Brother. Wherefore, to prevent the Survivor's untimely End, we'll presently send to see what Goods and Chattles the Deceased owns; and raising therewith another Rundlet of *Aqua-vitæ*, we'll privately bury our lately departed Brother, and drink his *Requiem*, without taking any farther Notice of this Disaster to our heretical Foes".

These were his Words as near as I can remember, and his Advice being applauded by all the Auditors, another Rundlet of *Aqua Vitæ* is fetc'd; but by that time it was near out, a fresh Quarrel arose, wherein a second Person was murder'd; which being likewise smother'd and a fresh Rundlet of *Aqua Vitæ* procur'd, I took my leave of these kind Heats, for fear they should at last raise a drunken Collation out of me. So I made the best of my way for *Foxford*, a very large Town, with a Church in it, lying among very high Hills. Hence I went to *Lorras*, an excellent Harbour for Ships, situated in a Bay, twining among exceeding high Mountains. Thence I went to *Sligo*, which hath a strong Citadel, by a Bridge containing Eight Stone Arches. Hence I went to *Grange*; from thence to *Balishannon*, a Seaport Town; hence I went to *Donnegal*, a Town situated on a Hill, and was burnt by the Duke of *Berwick*, in the late *Irish* Wars. Hence I went over *Barnsmoor*, a Mount Ten Miles in Length, in the Province of *Ulster*; but about a Mile before I came to the End of it, *Colcrockeda* [or the Hangman's] Wood begins; where a great many *Tories* or *Rapparees* have been hang'd, when they made their solitary Receptacles in this desolate and dangerous Place for robbing. Hence I went to *Rapho*, a Bishoprick, with a very little Church in it. And next I went to *London-Derry*, the People whereof have such good Stomachs as to eat Cats, Rats, Dogs and Horse-flesh in time of a Siege. The most remarkable Thing I saw hereabout was the Gallows, which stands about half a Mile out of Town, and is of a Triangular Form, like our Triple-Tree at *Hyde-Park* Corner; but as yet has not honour'd the *Roman* See with so many Saints and Martyrs as that in *England*.

From *London-Derry* I went to *Colrain*, a Seaport Town divided by the *Byrne* Water into Two Parts, so that it stands in the Counties of *Derry* and *Antrim*, which last Shire is much haunted with Fairies, who are so mischievous as to fling Darts at People as they Travel in the Night. I saw one of 'em, which is a flat solid Stone, about Two Inches long, and in Shape like a Vamp or upper Leather of a Woman's pecked Toe Shoe; one side white, t'other inclining to the same Colour, but speckled with red Spots; and is reckon'd very medicinal, if us'd according to Prescription, for the sore Teats of Cows. The *Irish* People, I perceiv'd all the Way I Travell'd, are haughty of Heart, implacable in Enmity; light of Belief, and patient *per* Force in Hunger and Cold. *Damage-fesant* is seldom committed, because here are few or no Hedges; nor can Forrest Laws be in much Use, when I saw not one from one End of the Kingdom to the other. Brogues are more worn than Shoes by both Sexes; their Mouths supply the Use of Bellows; a Pail of Water serves 'em for a Looking-Glass; and Cleanliness is as much unknown to them, as the Discoveries of *Christopher Columbus* to the Antients. The richer Sort of Women wear blue Cloth Cloaks, in all Weathers, as a Type or Symbol of their Desire of wearing the Breeches too; but their Husbands to mar their Intentions, generally wear Trowsers made of Frize, which is the staple Commodity of the Country. The midling Rank of Women wear Riding-Hoods; and the Poor ones clad themselves with course Mantles, thrown over their Kerchiefs, which are as black as their Bodies, and their Bodies as black as their Souls, but yet their Souls are blacker than either; if it was but for their Malice, contrary to the *11th* Commandment, commanding, *That ye love one another.*

Tho' the Women differ in their Habits, yet both Gentle and Simple count Decency in Dressing meer Idolatry; and that their Stockings may hang flatteringly about their Heels, they have utterly forsworn the Use of Garters. Those who are married are generally dull and sottish, so that when their Husbands come home, they look like so many Passion-Pictures, presenting ever Sadness and Melancholly; which makes the poor Cuckolds like *Spaniards*, who will leave their Saviour at any Time for a Maidenhead, look as dull. Yea, an *Irishman* loves a Whore as well as a *Frenchman*; and tho' the Superstition of former Times accounted a Woman of such Pollution, that the Council of *Eliberis* would not suffer a Man to touch her three Days before his receiving the Sacrament, yet in Defiance of all Councils, they will forsake Sacraments, and all things else holy, rather than go without a Bit of old Hat: And this Practice of abstaining from Women at certain Times, was (I suppose) in Use among the antient Heathens, according to this Caution of *Tibullus*.

> —— —— *discedat ab aris,*
> *Cui tulit hesterna gaudiis nocte Venus.*   L. 2. Eleg. 1.
>
> —— *From the Altars let him keep,*
> *That in his Lady's Arms last Night did sleep.*

By this Question in the last Chapter of *Proverbs*, as I take it, *Who can find a virtuous Woman?* One would be apt to surmise that *Solomon* had travell'd into this Country; and to see the People eat Clover Grass, a Man might swear 'em all a-kin to grazing *Nebuchadnezzar*. The Genius of the *Irish* is not a-whit admirable, for one Age here grows not wiser than another, like other Nations; which gives great Suspicion of a *Metempsischosis*, or *Pythagoras*'s Transmigration of the Soul to be true: Seeing, by the Conversation I had among the Bogtrotters, that the younger Folks only inherit the small Sense of their Progenitors; whose profound Knowledge was heretofore so great, as to tye Ploughs to their Horses Tails. Their Bogs are many, whence they have all their Fuel, for they burn nothing but Turf; Spiders are very plentiful, but not venomous; and the common Texture spun out of their Intrails, makes a Sort of Hangings, which the *Irish* for Cheapness prefer much before good Tapestry. In some Parts they make their Bread with the Bark of Holly, from which tearing off the green Superfluities, they work it up round like a Football, and bake it in the Embers. Their Butter being mixt with Salt and Garlick, and put into the Skin which follows the Calf from the Cow, they bury in a Turf-Pit for 8 or 9 Months together, which does not only make it of a strong Taste, but likewise dies it with all the Colours in the Rainbow: And Briskins, or the Roots of wild Tansie, they love as well. Tho' the Streets in every Town are very dirty, yet their Scavengers Carts are no bigger than Wheelbarrows; and the Use of Clogs or Pattins is an Abomination with most Women. The most epidemical Distemper among Strangers is the bloody Flux; for which, Eggs fry'd in Brandy is a good *Catholicon*. Few or no Patients happen among the lying-in Women; for (like the *Hebrews*, as their pious Midwives pretended) they are brought to Bed without any Help; wash and do all without Nurses; and in less than half a Week do not only go abroad, but also give Earnest for being with Child again. Their newborn Infants are as hardy, and will endure Cold as well as any *Laplander*; or the strongest Bear subject to the Czar of *Muscovy*. The *Irish* Soil mimicks Nature like the vivifying Mud of *Nile*; for I have seen the Hairs which fall from Horses Tails into Puddles of Water on the Road, transubstantiated (if I may be so bold as to use that Word, without any Offence to his Unholiness the Pope) into Worms; wherefore it is no Wonder that Priests, by the Art of *Legerdemain*, can convert good Bread and Wine into real Flesh and Blood.

Jack-Daws here are not black, but white and grey, like *Royston* Crows; and *Sea-Gulls* are all white, except their Wings, which are tipt at the End with a dark yellow; but the largest Birds in this Kingdom are *Whores-Birds* and *Jay!-Birds*. Here is a sort of Vermin breeding near Bogs call'd *Man-creepers*; in Shape and Bigness like a *Lizard*, having 4 Legs, the two foremost of which bear the Resemblance of a Human Hand. This Creature's Property is to creep into a Man's Belly, if he finds him sleeping with his Mouth open, where he extreamly tortures him, 'till fetch'd out of his internal Habitation; which Operation is thus perform'd. The Patient being kept fasting, his Chyrurgeon baits a Hook with a Piece of Meat, and puts it down his Throat, at which the hungry Insect snapping, he pulls him out with a sudden Jerk, and kills it. Milk will not keep (do what they can) from turning sour in six Hours at any time of the Year; but why this Region can't preserve this Sweetness longer, is somewhat paradoxical to me; unless the invisible *Effluvia*'s, which secretly dissipate themselves from the unwholsome Fogs, arising out of the Bogs, by the attractive Power of the Sun's Beams, assume the Prerogative of forcing the Putrefaction, so common to the liquid Product of the Cow's Teat. An *Ignis fatuus* the silly People deem to be a Soul broke out of *Purgatory*; and on the Vigil of St. *John* the *Baptist*'s Nativity they make Bonfires, and run along the Streets and Fields with Wisps of Straw blazing on long Poles to purify the Air, which they think infectious, by believing all the Devils, Spirits, Ghosts, and Hobgoblins fly abroad this Night to hurt Mankind. Farthermore, it is their dull *Theology* to affirm, the Souls of all People leave their Bodies on the Eve of this Feast, and take a Ramble to that very Place where, by Land or Sea, a final Seperation shall divorce them for evermore in this World. As soon as Death brings his last Summons to any one, the wild *Irish* (both Men, Women and Children) go before the Corpse, and from his or her House to the Church-yard set up a most hideous Holoo loo loo, which may be heard two or three Miles round the Country. Now when a Virgin (if here's any such Thing after she's in the Teens) dies, a Garland, made of all sorts of Flowers and sweet Herbs, is carried by a young Woman on her Head, before the Coffin, from which hang down two black Ribbons, signifying our mortal State; and two white, as an Emblem of Purity and Innocence; the Ends thereof are held by 4 young Maids, which are not so plenty here as *Thornbacks*, before whom a Basket full of Herbs and Flowers is supported by 2 other Maids, who strew them along the Streets to the Place of Burial: Then after the Deceased follow all her Relations, and Acquaintance. But the Priest being asham'd to walk without his *Pontificalibus*, he's as invisible, 'till you come to the Grave, as if he had the Ring of *Gyges* on his Finger.

Peas, Beans, and Artichoaks are very scarce; but what is worse, their Beef will not take Salt, without all the Fat melting away. The Inhabitants in general thinking Adultery and Fornication more laudable, than drawing the Picture of Posterity in the lawful State of Matrimony, the *Morbus gallicus* is as fashionable all over the Country, as in any Court in *Europe*; nevertheless, it is no Miracle to see them look fair to the last, since they drink nothing but what Nature's Liberality is pleas'd to bestow on 'em at Springs. Children that are troubled with Kibes are always in a sad Condition, because their poor Parents being great Strangers to any sort of salted Meat, they have no Brine to Cure them. When they use Phlebotomy they frequently bleed ill Blood, because it always runs in their Veins; and an *Apoplexy* seldom kills them, because they are not much pamper'd with high Feeding. A *Dropsie* does not much hurt an *Irishman*, by reason he naturally swells with his Rhodomontado's, and bragging Lies: But a deep *Consumption* always affects most their Pockets. Tho' all their Actions are evil, yet are they not much afflicted with the *King's-Evil*; nor are they much troubled with the *Gout*, because their Poverty does not qualifie them for it. I can't tell what an *Imposthume* may do, but a Lie will never choak them; nor do they seem to have the *Palsie*, but when a bad Conscience makes 'em quake and tremble like an Aspin Leaf: But indeed the People are all most grievously infected with the *Scurvy* and *Spleen* too. As for their Houses, the Rooms up one pair of Stairs, or higher, are cover'd with Earth 4 or 5 Inches thick; and the Tenent of the Joyces are not put into Mortises, but laid cross-wise into Notches over the Summet. An *Irishman* and Fool are Correlatives; or at least synonimous Terms: And catch him without a Blunder, which makes him love Bulls, 'tis to be fear'd the World is near its Dissolution. They speak largely of their Antiquity, boasting as if they were a People before the Creation; but, in my Opinion, *Ireland* could not well be *in esse* so early, because e'er a powerful *Fiat* produc'd all Things out of nothing, all Things lay in their original *Chaos*, so I can't imagine of what the *Irish* could exist, unless they derive their Descent from those *Atoms*, which by a casual Concourse (as the *Epicureans* hold) jumping together, gave Being to the World. Neither could it be a Country at the first Dawn of Light, by reason when Omnipotency had finisht his stupendious Works, he said, *they were good*; and the sacred Approbation was glorified by *all the Sons of the Morning, who shouted together for Joy*. Truly, I should rather impute the Original of this Country to some Judgment, which stirring up the Ocean, to overwhelm some remoter Part of the Globe, whose aggravating Sins too much incensed divine Justice, it left its antient Current, to make room for a Place as wicked: for you may read in divers Authors of a Resurrection of Isles, peeping up in many Parts, where none were ever seen before.

Their Language they do not only reckon older, but also more copious than the *Hebrew*; however, the Copiousness of their Linguo is easily guess'd at, by not having a Word in their Speech to express Breeches; and many other appellative

Words. Like the odious *French* they put the *Substantive* before the *Adjective*, and to embellish their Discourse, too often mixt with *Tautology*, they frequently use the Figure *Hysteron & Proteron*, that is, putting the Cart before the Horse. Their *Alphabet* contains but these 17 Letters, *A, B, C, D, E, F, G, I, L, M, N, O, P, R, S, T, U*; but this literal Paucity (like the *Saxon* Abecedary) is supply'd with some Abbreviations or Contractions. The Pronunciation of their Tongue being somewhat guttural, it is hard for the Vulgar to speak it; harder to speak it significantly; and hardest to write true. In the late King *James*'s Reign an *Irish* Teaguish Priest mightily extolling this Bogland Jargon, he as mightily interceeded with his papistick Majesty to erect publick Schools in *Oxford* and *Cambridge*, for professing this Tongue; but an *Irish* Courtier, who had no great Veneration for this conceited Pedlar in holy Trinkets, requesting the King to command him to translate, *Black Ox eat raw Egg*, the Priest presently perform'd his Talk thus, *Daue dooue ecye ewe ouce*; at which inarticulate Sounds (for if you was to hear them rightly pronounc'd, they sound just like a Dog's barking) his Majesty bursted out a laughing, and calling to his Dog *Towser*, said, *Here's my Dog can speak your Language already*; whereupon the spiritual Jugler drew in his Horns, and sneak'd off like a small Cur that had lost his Tail. In their Discourse it is common for them to use two Negatives, which I'm sure make an Affirmative; unless, after the manner of the *Greeks*, they use them to make the Negation stronger. It has been a great Dispute among *Grammarians*, whether an *Irishman* is a Noun *Substantive*, or a Noun *Adjective*; but it is carried in the latter, by reason he cannot stand by himself in Battle; for before the *Irish* go abroad, you shall not find greater Cowards under the Copes of Heaven.

Why the Men and Women here should be so unmercifully big in the Legs, above any other People, I impute to their mean Food, making no solid *Chyle*; so what slender Diet they eat, descending into their lower Parts, it there settles in a dropsical sort of a Humour. For all this Climate is reckon'd wholesome, it is rare to see any of the Natives past the climacterical Year; and their Perfidiousness is commonly attended with more Curses, in one respect or another, than are read in the *Commination* by our Clergy on *Ash Wednesday*. Such as have Pewter take great Delight to have it furbelow'd with Dust; and to wear clean Linnen they reckon as great a Crime as Loyalty. The People (like *Janus*) have not two Faces; but that they are double-hearted is confirm'd by the Votes of all moral Men: For thinking a sly deceiving their best Friends meritorious, is a general Rule they hold without any Exception. Here few Women die Martyrs for Love; but if they crave the Affections of a Man, wholly averse to their Inclination, their Endeavour to raise Enjoyment of him is by Art; and to this end they often use Philtres. Likewise, the Spark that's resolv'd to sacrifice his Youth and Vigour on a Damsel, whose Coyness will not accept of his Love-Oblations; he threads a Needle with the Hair of her Head, and then running it thro' the most fleshy Part of a dead Man, as the Brawn of the Arms, Thigh, or Calf of the Leg, the Charm has that Virtue in it, as to make her run mad for him whom she so lately slighted. Providence is very admirable in all its Dispensations, of strangely bringing surprising Accidents to pass; but more especially in *Ireland*, is her Gubernation of Chances wonderful, in preserving a People from starving, whose short Commons, in most Places, make a lively Representation of Famine. Their Skill in painting comes not near the rude Draughts of the boorish

Dutch; whose Fancy is more grotesque than natural: And their Churches discover neither any Workmanship after the old *Gothick* Fashion; nor shew the *Dorick, Corinthian,* or other Orders of modern Architecture. Also the Spaciousness of them may be soon guess'd at by their Cathedrals, the largest of which scarce exceeds *Oliver*'s Tabernacle, or *Calamy*'s *Presbyterian* Meeting-House in *Long Ditch* at *Westminster.*

This Country abounds with Foxes, and some wild Deer; Curlues and Cuckolds; and many Rooms in most Houses having no Chimnies, one would take every Town to be a Vent of Mount *Ætna*, when the Smoak (which is enough to stifle *Charon*) makes the Walls as black as Hell: And because *Sarah* was buried in the Field of *Macpelah,* some of the *Irish* have the Ambition to be buried in open Places. The People are so alike for Rags and Jags, that I believe *Plautus* took his *Amphitryo* from them.

From *Colrain* I went to *Antrim*, thence to *Belfast*, and thence to *Donaghadea,* where you may dine at 12 at Noon, and by Water get to *Port Patrick* in *Scotland,* by 3 in the Afternoon. It being natural for the *Irishmen* to be as Jealous as *Spaniards,* from whom they pretend to be descended, they will not let their Wives wear Smocks, to prevent their Neighbours from taking up their Linnen; and if a Man has a great Estate here, he cannot with the *Psalmist* say, *My Liues are fallen to me in pleasant Places.* The Hazel Wood in *Ireland* is obnoxious to Snakes, which expire in the Circles made with them; nor will a Toad, or any other venomous Creature, live in this Clime: But the Reason why the Soil is so blest, is because the People are curst.

THE COMICAL PILGRIM'S PILGRIMAGE INTO HOLLAND.

eturning from *Ireland* to *England* again, and being still of a roving Mind, I was dispos'd to go to *Holland*, I think it was on the longest Day in the Year, call'd *Barnaby* bright, when going down to *Margate* in the Isle of *Thanet*, where *Austin* the Monk landed to convert *Kentish* Infidels, I went on board the *Swiftsure*, a third Rate Man of War, on which Admiral *Shovel* had hoisted his Flag, in his convoying King *William* then over to *Holland*. A fair Wind favouring us, we soon arriv'd upon the Coast of *Holland*, which I perceiv'd was so low, that the People had the Advantage of other Nations, for if they die in Perdition, they have a shorter Cut to Hell than the rest of their Neighbours.

I landed at the *Briel* in the Isle of *Voorne*, where is good Accommodation enough for Travellers, but only they pay dear for it. Hence I cross'd over the *Maes* River to the Isle of *Roosenburg*, for 5 Stivers; and for 3 more I cross'd over for *Vlaerding*, and by that Time I got thither, I found the Ground so light all the way, that a strong Earthquake would shake the whole 17 Provinces of the *Netherlands* into a *Chaos*. Most of their Dwellings in this Town, as well as other Places, stand like Privies in moated Houses, hanging still over the Water; and had St. *Stephen* been condemn'd to suffer here, he might have been alive this Day; for unless it be their paved Cities, Gold is a little more plentiful than Stones; except it be living ones, and then for their Heaviness you may take in almost all the Nation. It is a singular Place to fat Monkies in, for there are Spiders as fat as Shrimps; and a starting Horse endangers you two Deaths at once, breaking your Neck and drowning. *Holland* hanging most in the Water, it seems but a Bridge of swimming Earth; and if *Ætna* be the Mouth or fore Gate of Hell, surely here is found the Postern, where the full Earth doth vent her crude black Gore, which the Inhabitants do scrape away for Fuel, as Men with Spoons do Excrements from Civit Cats. They dress their Meat *in Aqua cælesti*, for it springs not as ours from the Earth, but comes to them as *Manna* to the *Israelites* falling from Heaven. This they keep under Ground 'till it stinks, and then they pump it out again for Use; So when you wash your Face with one Hand, you had need hold your Nose with the other; for tho' it be not a Cordial, yet is it certainly a strong Water; and an *English* Bailiff prefers it far beyond *Mint* Water. Their Ditches they distinguish into Nooks, as my Lord Mayor's Cook does his Custards; and every *Dutchman* being his own Herald, Escutcheons are as plentiful among the Boors as Gentry is scarce.

From *Vlaerding* I went to *Schiedam*, a small Town abounding in Fishery; and where Abundance of Busses, Cord, and Network is made. Here entring a House, the first Thing (as in other Houses) I encounter'd was a Looking-Glass and next other Utensils of a Family, marshalled about the Room like so many Watch-men. Were the Knacks of all their Houses set together, they would far exceed the Trumpery of *Deard*'s Toyshop in *Fleet-street*, or the Court of Requests; and if you want to speak *Dutch*, you may learn a great deal from their Signs, for what they are they always write under them. Coaches and Carts are as rare as Comets; and all their Merchandize they draw through the Streets on Sledges, as we do our Traytors on Hurdles to *Tyburn*. Their Rooms being but as so many Sand-Boxes, you must either go out to spit, or blush when you see the Mop brought. As their Beds require a Ladder or Stairs to get into 'em, you are in Danger of breaking your Neck if you tumble out; and as they keep their Houses cleaner than their Bodies, so do they take Care to have their Bodies cleaner than their Souls. They are not so nice-conscioned, but that they can turn out Religion to let in Policy; and a *Dutch* Woman, being the Head of the Husband, she takes the Horn to her own Charge, which she often multiplies, and bestows the Increase on her Man. The People are generally boorish, therefore their Country is the God they Worship, War is their Heaven, Peace is their Hell, and the *Spaniard*, the Devil they hate.

From *Schiedam* I went to *Rotterdam*, the second great Emporium of this trading People, situated on the Side and Banks of the *Maes*, and fitted for all Conveniency of Transport and Importation. Here, as in other Places, I found I might sooner convert a *Jew*, than make a *Dutchman* yield to Arguments that cross him, because his Spirits are generated from *English* Beer; and his Body is built of pickled Herring, which makes him testy. If you see him fat, he hath been rooting in a Cabbage Ground, and that bladder'd him; he is as churlish as his Breeder *Neptune*; and the Love of Gain is as natural to him, as Water to a Goose, or Carrion to any Kite. Truth and Honesty is as scarce here as Hedges; they are seldom deceiv'd, because they trust no Body; and Complement is an Idleness they were never train'd in. They shall abuse a Stranger for nothing; and after a few base Terms scotch one another to a Carbanado. All that help them not, they hold popish; and take it for an Argument of much Honesty, to rail bitterly against the King of *Spain*. Every thing is so made to swim among them, that it is a Question if *Elijah*'s Ax were now floating there, whether it would be taken for a Miracle. The Shipping is the *Babel* which they boast on for the Glory of their Nation; and they are in a manner all *Aquatiles*, and therefore the *Spaniards* call them Water-Dogs. A *Turkish* Man of War is as dreadful to them as a Falcon to a Mallard, from whom their best Remedy is to steal away; and Sailors among 'em, are as common as Beggars with us, besides the *Dutch* Tarpaulins will drink, rail, swear, niggle, steal, and be lousie alike. Slime, humid Air, Water, and wet Diet, have so bagg'd their Cheeks, that some would take their Paunches to be gotten above their Chins; and bring under a democratical Government, tell them of a King in Jest, and they will cut your Throat in Earnest;

for they hate the Name of Majesty more than a *Jew* doth Images, a Woman pure Virtue, or a Nonconformist a Surplice; and it is reported that there is but a Sheet of Paper betwixt *Rotterdam* and Hell, which is a nearer Way to old Nick than by *Rochester*.

From *Rotterdam* I went to *Delf*, where I observ'd that every *Mynheer* shall walk the Streets as Usurers go to Bawdy-Houses, all alone and melancholly; and their Apparel is civil enough, but very uncomely, as having usually more Stuff than Shape. *Holland* is the Fair of all Sects, where all the Pedlars of Heresies have Leave to vent their Toys, their Ribbands, and fanatick Rattles. They will admit of all Religions but the true one; and whosoever disturbs the civil Government shall be liable to Punishment, but the Decrees of Heaven and Sanctions of Deity, any one may break uncheck'd, by professing what false Religion he pleases. The Men are cladded tolerably well, unless he inclines to the Sea-Fashion; and then are his Breeches yawning at the Knees, as if they were about to swallow up his Legs. The *Dutch* Women have much more Forehead than Face; and they are starch'd so blue, that if they once grow old, you would verily believe you saw *Winter* walking up to the Neck in Indigo; They are far from going naked, for of a whole Woman you can see but half a Face; her Hand shews her to be a sore Labourer; and if you look lower, she's like a Monkey chain'd about the Middle, and had rather want it in Diet, than not have Silver Hooks to hang her Keys in. Their Smocks are ever whiter than their Skin; and their Gowns are fit to hide great Bellies; but they make them shew so unhandsome, that *Englishmen* don't care for getting them. Where the Women lies in, the Ringle or Knocker of the Door does Pennance, for it is lapped round about with Linnen, either to show you that loud Knocking may wake the Child, or else that for a Month her Ring is not to be run at. For their Diet they eat much and spend little; and when they send out a Fleet to the *East-Indies*, it shall live 3 Months on the Offals, which we fear would surfeit our Swine; yet they feed on't, and are still the same *Dutchmen*. In their Houses, Roots and Stockfish are staple Commodities; and if they make a Feast, and add Flesh, they have an Art to keep it hot more Days, than a dirty, dingy, greasie Cook a Pig's Head in *Pye-Corner*.

The *Dutch* Women are delivered, together with their Children, of a *Sooterkin*, not unlike to a Rat, which some imagine to be the Offspring of the Stoves they have betwixt their Legs in Winter. Their Fairs are more frequented on *Sundays* in the Afternoon, than their Churches in the Forenoon; and they are furnish'd with such a wonderful Plenty of Corn by their Neighbours; that they have not only enough for their own Use, but also to export sufficiently to other Countries, by selling them at an extravagant Price a Pig of their own Sow. There is no Nation in the World whose Seas yield the like constant and general Benefit as our Seas do; wherefore the Sloth of the *English* may very well be blam'd, for suffering the *Dutch* under their Noses, to rob them of that Wealth, which would be theirs at the small Rate of an easie Industry. But tho' all the Commodities they have either domestick or foreign, their fishing in our Seas brings them in the greatest Profit, yet have they another Commodity which is very profitable to them, and that is War; for whereas other Nations are undone by it, they have the Secret to thrive, and grow exceeding rich by it. The Innholders paying as much for the Excise of Victuals and Drink, as they did at first for the Thing, it makes the *Entrata* or Revenue of those High and Mighty States (who, when they implor'd Queen *Elizabeth's* Aid, writ themselves the poor, distressed States of *Holland*) very considerable. This free State entertaining all Renegadoes, it is the common Sink of Villany; each Faction calls itself a Church; and every new-fangled, giddy-headed, enthusiastical Botcher, Cobler, or Tinker, is able enough to sow Sedition: But the general Religion here is *Calvanism*, the Profession whereof, tho' fatal to Monarchical Government, agrees well enough with the Parity of free States, where the People have so much Voice and Authority.

Holland, with the 16 other Provinces is call'd the *Low-Countries*, and the *Netherlands*, from their low Situation. Here live almost as many, if not more, *Jews*, *Anabaptists*, *Socinians*, and *Papists*, as *Calvanists*; so that a Traveller who comes hither, need not want a Religion to choose which shall best please him. Whilst I was in *Rotterdam*, being one Night in Company with some of the *Dutch* Boors, who were extolling *Erasmus*, who was born in that Town, for the greatest Scholar the World ever bred, my Blood broil'd at their Insolence, as knowing *England*, and other Nations have produc'd Men of better Learning, but they being too many for me to resent it, I had no other Way to vent my Resentment, but by writing the following Lines, which I privately stuck upon his Effigies cast in Brass, and erected not far from the House where he was born.

> *Thou great* Colossus! *if you stood astride,*
> *Betwixt thy Legs the* Dutchmen *post might ride*
> *To tell,* Erasmus *is the only Boor,*
> *Whom they for Learning brag of and adore.*
> *Great were thy nat'ral and acquired Parts,*
> *Which made you ign'rant in the Lib'ral Arts;*
> *And tho' thou wert half Fool, and half a Knave,*
> *Half* Protestant, *and yet to* Rome *a Slave,*
> *Thy Doctrine serv'd this People very well,*
> *Who here are damn'd, before they're damn'd in Hell.*
> *So farewel solid, monumental Brass,*
> *Erected to commemorate an Ass.*

But the high and mighty States being affronted at this Lampoon put upon their chief Priest, a Proclamation was issued forth, promising the Reward of 500 Guilders for apprehending the Author of it; whereupon I fled to *Delph* in the twinckling of a Bed-Staff. This is a pretty round compacted Town, about 2 Miles in Circumference, fortified with a strong Wall and Ditch, but after an old Fashion; and is the great Magazine and Armory of the Commonwealth, which is democratical, as I said before, for Monarchy they abhor as much as a *Scotchman* does *Episcopacy*, or a true bred *Irishman* paying Allegiance to a *Protestant* Prince.

From *Delph* I went to the *Hague*, the Metropolis of *Holland*, not for Trade, but for the States assembling at this Place, which is round compacted, and neatly built: It is neither Town nor City, but call'd a Village, as being unwall'd, and is reckon'd the biggest in the World. Within half a League of this Place lies interr'd in an Abby *Margaret* Countess of *Henenberg*, Sister to *William*, King of the *Romans*, and on her Tomb still remains an Epitaph, which mentions, that she brought forth as many

Children at one Birth, as are Days in the Year. The Country has few Trees in it, because the Ground is so waterish and soft, that it is not able to bear the Weight of one; and for the same Reason a less Quantity of Fruit and Grain grows in it.

Their chiefest Fuel is Turf, of which they burn so much, that it may be very well thought the *Dutch* will burn up their own Land before the Day of Judgment They are so cumbred about the Affairs and Business of this World, that their Ignorance in Religion is unaccountable. The Theological Terms of Regeneration, Consubstantiality, Predestination, Justification, Sanctification, or hypostatical Union, are full as mysterious to them, as the intricate Hierogliphics of the antient *Egyptians* were to the Vulgar. 'Tis true, they nevertheless keep the *Sabbath-Day* very strict, for all the while that divine Service in their blind way holas, they do no manner of Work but wash in the open Streets, keep Shops almost open, angle, sing, play on the Musick, dance, drink, and whore; for as six Days are tiresome to be at hard Labour, their high Mightinesses allow the People one Day in seven to go to the Devil with Pleasure. In five, the *Dutch* are good for nothing but to be serv'd as a Sultan or Grand Seignior once advis'd a French King, which advice was to send an Army of Pioneers to dig up their Country, and throw all the Inhabitants at once into the Sea.

FINIS.

Lector House believes that a society develops through a two-fold approach of continuous learning and adaptation, which is derived from the study of classic literary works spread across the historic timeline of literature records. Therefore, we aim at reviving, repairing and redeveloping all those inaccessible or damaged but historically as well as culturally important literature across subjects so that the future generations may have an opportunity to study and learn from past works to embark upon a journey of creating a better future.

This book is a result of an effort made by Lector House towards making a contribution to the preservation and repair of original ancient works which might hold historical significance to the approach of continuous learning across subjects.

HAPPY READING & LEARNING!

LECTOR HOUSE LLP
E-MAIL: lectorpublishing@gmail.com